MW00944329

Transforming Childhood Trauma

8 Steps To Reclaim Your Life

David Brady, MFA

DEDICATION

Dedicated with Love to My Children Andrew, Colleen, Brendan and Laurel and to my wonderful and amazing grandkids Sophie, Guerin, Henry and Conlan

"Your are My Inspiration"

CONTENTS

ACKNOWLEDGMENTS

I want to thank Sonny Goldstein for his friendship and support. I couldn't have done this without you.

I want to thank two of my oldest friends in the world, Mike O'Shea and Brian Rogers for their undying support and kindness.

Thanks to my pals Kumar, Bert, Peter and Tom and Dr. Mike for being willing to give me honest feedback.

Thanks to my Master Mind partners, Mike, Barb, Jey, Carollyne and Roy.

A very special thanks to my old friends Alan Vogeler, George Flak, Richard Landry, Johnny Brower and Jim Goodrich

1 FOREWORD

"The Buck Stops Here"

President Harry Truman

The book is not a book about assigning blame or avoiding responsibility for how my life turned out.

I wrote it with the goal that you, the reader, might find hope in these pages and discover that there is a solution to any and all the problems, pain and challenges you may be facing in life if you too have come out of an alcoholic, addiction based, or dysfunctional family.

Perhaps there wasn't alcohol or substance abuse issues, but there may have been emotional, physical, spiritual or sexual abuse in your background.

Like our family, yours too may have looked picture perfect on the outside. We lived in a beautiful house, my mother, thank God, was sane and caring. But my father was an out of control daily drinker who exhibited total disregard for our well being once he picked up a drink. Sober, you couldn't meet a nicer man.

You may have recreated your family of origin in your current relationship. You may have married an alcoholic or drug addict, or you may have found someone who is not only not reliable but has abandoned or abused you in much the same way your parent/s did. You may have developed a drinking or drug problem yourself, or you may have become a compulsive overeater, gambler, sex addict or love addict. You may be a chronic worrier, afraid that your life will never work out.

You may be a massive overachiever, and while the world looks at you as an amazing success, you may feel like a complete fraud. You may be full of fear being discovered by your employer, partner or friends. You may feel alone and isolated even in a room full of friends.

The good news is you are no longer alone. It is my heartfelt wish that what you find within these pages would help you to find some answers.

No one should ever feel shame or guilt for admitting that life is often tough, and we all need help from time to time to get through it. I would feel I've succeeded if what I've written here could assist you along your journey find some of the answers to life's trials. For me, the beginning of feeling better was to change the context of trouble. It wasn't horrible— it was firming up on the downside.

When I was in graduate school, my intention was to become and alcohol and drug counselor. Then I made my first film, Alcohol, Drugs and the Young in British Columbia with the Royal Canadian Mounted Police. That experience changed the direction of my life one hundred and eighty degrees, and I became a filmmaker instead.

I have written extensively on the subject of chemical addiction, codependency as well as a plethora of addictive behaviors for a television series titled Meeting The Crisis, the 12 Step Approach.

During that time, I read and studied the literature of Alcoholics Anonymous as well as Alanon (for families of Alcoholics) and especially Adult Children of Alcoholics and Codependents Anonymous for that series.

All of those programs work off of the twelve steps of Alcoholics Anonymous. The late Aldous Huxley once called Bill Wilson, the co-founder of Alcoholics Anonymous "the greatest social architect" of the 20th century.

This book is not a substitute for any of those programs. They all offer incredible support and a very safe environment to find a solution for those who want a ready-made community of recovering people. This book is an addition to that literature, which has helped countless millions of individuals and families recover from both alcoholism and the family disease of alcoholism.

Today, The American Medical Association recognizes addiction as a disease. Codependency is recognized by many therapists and frontline workers in the field of alcoholism and addiction to be the core issue underlying many of these conditions.

Many believe codependency and most addiction are the direct results of trauma. I think all of these abnormal conditions are like type-two diabetes; they can be arrested, but seldom if ever cured.

What sets this book apart is that I have written it from my point of view and experience. I have successfully confronted my demons due to growing up in a violent, alcoholic home. I have also successfully dealt with my alcohol and drug problems and have lived a life free of all mood-altering substances for three decades. What I was to discover was that just stopping drinking was not necessarily the answer to my problems that I thought were creating the difficulties in my life.

Initially, how I dealt with the effects of growing up in an alcoholic family is I became a massive overachiever. I swore I would not be my father and expose my children to the kind of insanity I was through my father's use of alcohol.

For the record, I am a successful feature film and television writer, producer, and director. I have taught at three of Canada's universities and was the recipient of the CESAR Teaching Award at Ryerson University in Toronto, Canada. I am a classic over-achiever.

I was blessed with a great deal of success, and more blessed with what I thought was crushing failure.

All of these experiences have contributed in significant ways to my life. Out of my greatest failures have come my biggest successes. Ironically, my biggest successes have been quite empty and meaningless. I know that sounds paradoxical, but it is true. I spent the first thirty-nine years of my life pursuing material and creative success, and the next twenty-five seeking enlightenment. I'm hoping to spend the time I have left of my life giving—whenever and wherever I can. It is better to give than to receive.

This book doesn't fit into any particular genre. It is part self-help, part autobiographical, part observational and part inspirational (I hope). I've written it as I speak—as if I was sharing with you, one on one.

When I was brought to my knees in 1986, I owed five million dollars, and was facing hundreds of lawsuits against me from a feature film I was producing in the United States. I will explain more about that situation later. It was at this point that I once said to a friend, " I think it's always darkest before the bottom falls out." I have a twisted sense of humor that has served me well in life, and I will touch on it at various times throughout my writings.

What I have discovered is that learning can often involve pain. I have come to see that pain can be a very positive experience.

If you are baffled by that statement, I don't blame you. But think about it: not only does pain tell us to seek medical help when we don't feel well physically, but it also urges us to seek emotional relief when we feel overwhelmed by life.

I am a believer in the old saying; Religion is for those afraid of going to hell; spirituality is for those of us who've been there.

The first chapters of this book describe my life in a general way and, I hope, will give you a glimpse of the psychological and emotional landscape of my childhood. I have shared the detail I have so there will be no question in your mind that I don't know what I am talking about. Some of my stories are somewhat personal, and my mind rails against me exposing myself like this as it would be very easy to criticize me for my behavior when I succumbed to addiction in my early years. I pray you won't judge me too harshly.

The latter half of the book is drawn from my experience working a variety of spiritual practices. They include the eight steps of the Master Mind Principles, developed by the late Jack Boland, a Unity minister. I also draw on academic disciplines I acquired over the years.

I sincerely hope that you will find value in the eight steps of the Master Mind Principles. They were Jack's way of stating that when two or more are gathered, then God is there too. I want to say here that while I was raised Roman Catholic, I am not a practicing Roman Catholic. But my beliefs are much less orthodox and much more inclusive of many other beliefs.

I know there is a God, it just isn't me– at this point in my life. All I know and believe today is that God does exist. I use the term God frequently throughout this book, but I want to emphasize this point. It is the God of your understanding, and no one is trying to convince you that you have to believe in anything within the pages of this book. These are suggestions only.

But what my research in comparative religions showed is that there is a common bond or root to most of the world's modern religions, whether we are looking at Christianity, Judaism or Islam. They have a lot more in common than they do differences.

I cannot emphasize this point enough: to gain benefit from what I am about to share with you, you do not have to believe in any formal or traditional religion. You don't have to be any specific denomination or faith to have this work for you. Nor am I trying to sell you on the concepts or theology contained in them.

They were the simplest, most straightforward plan of action I could find that helped me in overcoming particular personal, behavioral, emotional and financial challenges, which I faced and thought were insurmountable as a result of growing up in a dysfunctional alcoholic home.

Today I can see the cause of almost all of my problem's direct roots go back to my childhood and the decisions I made based on erroneous self-defeating thinking and beliefs from those early years.

If you are looking for an empirical or dialectic discussion on whether God exists or not, then I would suggest Hans Kung's, Does God Exist? I only spend a brief time describing my belief and acceptance of God, as I understand God to be.

There is no doubt in my mind, and the difference between an atheist and me is that I've been where they are, but few have ever been where I am. You can believe in any higher power you choose, including your local hydro or power provider, and still participate in these spiritual exercises. It doesn't matter what your faith

2. CRASH & BURN

In August of 1986, I was basking in the glow of three very successful and exciting film projects. First was the nomination of my then-associate Phillip Borsos's documentary film, Nails, for an Academy Award. Second was executive producing Till Death Do Us Part, a small feature film that received very favorable reviews in "Variety", The Toronto Star and from many of the critics in Canada and the United States. The highlight was executive producing The Grey Fox, an independent feature film starring the late Richard Farnsworth. Francis Ford Coppola's Zoetrope Studios presented the film. United Artists Classics released it. The Grey Fox received worldwide critical acclaim and commercial success. The Grey Fox won seven Genies, (Canadian Academy

Awards) and nominated for two Golden Globes for Best Foreign Picture and Best Actor for Richard Farnsworth. We were on a roll.

Buoyed by these successes, I began producing another feature film in The Untied States. Originally titled Indian Summer,

it morphed into Dixie Lanes. While the cast and crew were incredible, the film lacked a creative and critical cohesion. I accept responsibility for those deficiencies.

Before Dixie Lanes, and while working on my previous three successful films I was creatively soaring. What no one knew except for those closest to me is I was personally descending into a void fueled by an addiction to Bolivian Marching Powder. It was akin to riding the head of an unguided ballistic missile.

The trajectory up was rapid, as was the descent into the dark night of the soul.

However, I thought Dixie Lanes

would be the opportunity for me to turn my life around and live "clean and sober and happily ever after," as the movies say. I had been clean six months when I started it. Ironically, I had not had a drink at that point since I was 22 years of age—in other words, 17 years. Apparently, just quitting drinking had not solved my problems.

This book is not about the demise of Dixie Lanes, my career or my finances. It is an examination of the journey upon which Dixie Lanes was to propel me, so I could make sense of what happened to me—why, after three previous successes over a seven-year period, did I choose a project that ended in such disaster?

The catalyst that propelled me forward was created by the problems I was having with the financing of the film. I had taken two Washington State towns and turned them back to the 1940s—then had to leave them there. The financing I was counting on and paid for never appeared in our bank account. We were the victims of commercial fraud. I ended up personally owing $4 million U.S., which was over $5 million Canadian at the time, and I believed in my heart of hearts that I was going to be able to pull off a miracle, just like we had so many times before, and pay everyone off.

I thought, if I, at least, got the film finished, chances were I could recoup enough from it to achieve that goal. If I shut it down, there was zero chance of recovering anything, and we would be out over $1 million of our money. The Grey Fox had run out of money. So had Till Death Do Us Part.

Every night, for almost three months, I would go up to my motel room, shut the door and go into a state of shock from fear. There was no one I could talk to because everyone was counting on me to keep the picture going. Every morning before I went downstairs to start another day of shooting, I would go to the bathroom and throw up from fear.

I know from personal experience what it is like to lose everything, to face massive public criticism and to face an economic recession – and in this case, a self-created financial depression.

I survived and came away more prosperous, peaceful and more purposeful than I've ever been, and I learned how to make my life manageable, keep my word and reclaim my life in spite of what appeared to be an impossible situation. In an odd way, at a micro level, my life emulated what is going on in the world today at a macro level. I had allowed greed, self-centeredness and ego (edge good/God out) to take over my life.

At the time, I just thought I was doing what I had been told by my father would make me successful—and, I assumed, happy. Wrong again! I hate that.

Here is what I believed, and what I had been told: make a lot of money, gain a lot of attention, acquire a beautiful home and an equally impressive car and a beautiful woman—or flip the order in whichever way you want. I had all of those things in spades. I had met a few wonderful women over a seven-year period, acquired a beautiful home on the Pacific Ocean in West Vancouver, shared a beach house in Malibu with my old friend John Brower, and rented an apartment overlooking the East River in Manhattan and a beautiful townhouse in Toronto.

I constantly moved between these four residences. Deep down, I felt that it was hard to hit a moving target because I didn't want anyone getting too close to me.

I was just reminded, on a telephone call from my friend and attorney Bob Rosenblatt about my friend Jim's yacht that he'd gotten with another friend in New York City, that I ended up living there in 1984, on Jerome Kern's old Showboat – a 74-foot yacht. So the lack of material resources was not my problem. It was recklessly borrowing the money to keep that wild lifestyle up.

I find that life is often full of ironies. During that period, I went to my old friend, the respected Canadian journalist Jim Purdy and told him, "I feel nervous about Dixie Lanes. I expect they're going to run at me in the papers." He laughed in his quiet Scottish brogue and dismissed the whole notion with his hand. "You're worried about nothing," he said. "Nobody cares about you or your film."

The very next week, the New York Times published an article with a large headline "The Film That Bounced." The Seattle paper ran an ongoing series of front-page articles for a week. In its early days, CNN covered the story.

I was sitting in my apartment in Toronto when the phone rang and an associate from New York was visiting Germany said, "I just saw you on CNN." At home, The Globe and Mail, Canada's national daily newspaper picked up the story.

Jim had me look at the bright side. He pointed out that you couldn't buy this kind of publicity with a million dollars. Too bad I wasn't in the market for any at that period of my life.

In addition to the $4 million U.S. that

I owed personally, I had approximately 605 lawsuits launched against me. It was not just the dark night of the soul, it had moved up to bleak, barren hopelessness, and I had nowhere to turn. There is no way to describe adequately the feelings I had at that time. As I previously mentioned, fear ran rampant. I couldn't sleep at night. I was filled with an impending sense of doom and a real sense of despondency.

I felt entirely alone. I felt abandoned. I had a sensation of sinking— like I was drowning in a sea of emotion that I had no control over. My mind raced uncontrollably creating scenarios of possible catastrophes in my mind (none of which came to pass by the way.) Then it dawned on me.

I was either going to kill myself, or crawl out of the hole I'd dug, which originally had functioned as my shelter in my childhood to survive living in an insane alcoholic home. What had happened is that I had built an impenetrable wall around myself for self-protection, only now, as an adult, I couldn't break through the barriers I had erected to protect myself.

When I went back to Jim Purdy, he pointed out that this kind of publicity was worth its weight in gold and not to pay any attention to what the papers had written. We both laughed about it years later when I got over the humiliation of the experience. That's when I realized people were so self-obsessed that they didn't care a week or month later what had been written about us. It was my late associate, Phillip Borsos, who was to take me off the front page when his film, Bethune, was experiencing tremendous difficulties shooting in China. The headline in the Toronto Star read "Let them Eat Dog Meat," referring to a comment by the Chinese officials reacting to the Canadian crew's complaint about the lack of proper food.

When Phil arrived home from China, I called and thanked him for unintentionally helping me out.

He was the one who suggested I should turn the negative over to the State if

I couldn't come up with the money to pay the creditors.

As a result of that experience, I began to question every aspect of my life. Why did I live in a perpetual state of fear: fear of the future, fear of failure, fear of success, and fear of financial insecurity? When I had these overwhelming feelings, why did I insist on living out on the edge like I did? In my bravado, I used to say I had no fear of debt, but I was terrified of creditors.

I also wondered why, in spite of all the success I'd had, did I have such low self-esteem? I could never feel how others looked on the outside: confident, gregarious and well put together. Others saw me as a success, but I couldn't. I felt like a fraud.

No matter how well I did, my mind would tell me I could have done it better. Why did I constantly blame others for my troubles? It was not the first time I had sabotaged myself.

The moment I accepted that we were

out of money on the film Dixie Lanes and had no hope of any, I knew my life as I'd led it was over. I also thought my career was, too. The film wasn't finished, and I was starting to think it never would be.

I didn't follow the business advice that was suggested and declare bankruptcy. I felt if I did, I would never learn whatever it was I had to learn about managing my finances and my life. Nor would I get to the cause of why my life was out of control, financially and emotionally. If I didn't take a stand and confront myself about why I'd acted and behaved the way I had, chances were I would find myself right back in the same position again. In this case, once was enough, and I'm grateful to say it has been.

Finding the answers to why my life was so unmanageable has been a long, slow process that is still underway today. Initially, I struggled every day to stay in the game. I was incredibly depressed and wondered if I would ever be able to start overcoming any of the difficulties I was facing. I owed so much money; I didn't know where to start. Finally, after four years of very intense personal work, I began sending out payments of five dollars to various individuals that I owed thousands or hundreds of thousands of dollars. Before that, it was always just talking and empty promises. At least with five dollars, it was a real concrete action.

One lawyer in New York said I restored his faith in humanity. In the last few years the payments have risen significantly, but with so many people, I needed to generate a significant amount of cash to make the final payments possible.

I also had to prioritize my creditors. There is a whole group I've never even begun to repay. I was told to take care of the people who stood by me through the difficult years first. This is where I still am today. It was suggested to then care of the trade creditors of the corporation because, while I don't have a legal obligation, I feel a moral one to make them as whole as I possibly can. For my original commitments, I was able to sell off individual assets I owned, such as screenplays, video rights and revenues from the film, to reduce the production debt to a more manageable level. I have never personally realized another penny from this movie.

The Attorney General for the State of Washington investigated my production company. Our financial records confirmed we had paid twenty-five thousand US dollars (nearly $55,0000 in today's dollars) to a New York law firm as the last step to satisfy all of the conditions necessary to close on the financing of the film.

The New York lawyer had represented to my US Attorney, and me that the money I was seeking was already on deposit, and all we had to do was pay him, and our film was financed.

We paid, and the check was cashed, but no money ever materialized. Live and learn.

We had another executive producer

who was unable to raise all the necessary funds. But it was not for a lack of trying.

Dixie Lanes was a horrific, humiliating experience for me. I have never felt so much pain, except for my childhood, from that experience of failing. But out of pain comes growth—tremendous growth. I couldn't see it then, but in retrospect, Dixie Lanes gave me my life back. No one could have told me that at the time, however.

Perhaps you haven't lost millions of dollars, but you might have lost your job or your company as a result of the recent economic downturns. Maybe you were one of the one's who lost your home during the housing crisis a decade ago. Perhaps you are on the verge of losing your house or your car right now. Maybe you've found yourself with a substance abuse issue. Or, you might be facing bankruptcy, or your husband or wife or partner may be walking out on you because you have difficulty forming a long-standing relationship.

Possibly, you live in constant fear and dread about the future. You may still be reeling from the effects connected to this financial meltdown with major banks and corporations that we never believed could ever be in trouble. We lose sleep wondering about our pension funds as these companies teeter on the verge of collapse and wondering, what in God's name is going on in the world?

Perhaps you are still awestruck by the events of over fifteen years ago created by the attacks of September 11th or the wars in Iraq and Afghanistan – the recent emergence of ISIS. How can these horrible events take place? Are you terrified for the well-being of your children or your parents? You may worry that our whole society is coming apart at the seams Perhaps you have doubts about your abilities.

I know that I experienced many of these feelings and emotions, and have had the same questions racing through my mind at various times. Today, I feel as if my life has been utterly changed. It doesn't mean I still don't feel angry and resentful from time to time, or I don't have bad days.

I am no longer as powerless over my emotions and my fears as I once was. I am no longer run by my thoughts about the future all he time. I do have peace of mind a great deal of the time. I also have a life I could never have dreamt possible in the past.

I was married for nearly twenty years, and when my wife and I split, it was done with love and compassion for both of us. I have regained the love of my son from my first marriage and reconciled with my oldest daughter and her family. I have found the ability to forgive myself for my past mistakes. I have been able to set right the majority of those relations in my past where I hurt others—especially my family and friends.

At present, I live in a few places. First is at a beautiful house I have on the Bay of Quinte, in Eastern Ontario. I have a nice place in Vancouver. My country house is a stone's throw from the Thousand Islands, and in a short drive, I can glance across the St. Lawrence in Upstate New York.

I like to walk on the sea wall in Vancouver or sit on my deck and watch the seasons pass—each one more beautiful than the next. I am happy 80 percent of the time. I also have a mind that, when I'm in the 20 percent downturn, tells me I will always feel that way. My mind lies to me. That's why today when my mind starts to chatter about all that is going on in the world, I just thank it for sharing.

So, how in the hell did I end up in such a mess you ask? You might say I had an unhappy childhood—only it lasted 39 years. Embarrassing to admit. But true.

3. THE CHILDHOOD YEARS

Timmins, Ontario. Today it is known as the home of Shania Twain, but in the 1950s, it was home to my family and me. The town was built on a large hill of solid rock, surrounded by thousands of square miles of rugged wilderness made up of spruce, balsam and pine trees mixed with cedar forests. A distinct, fresh, fragrant scent of evergreens pervades Northern air. At night, the skies are so clear and bright you feel as if you could almost touch the stars. Often the Northern Lights shine majestically over the far-off horizon, dancing in the sky.

Timmins came into being near the turn of the twentieth century and contained the second-richest gold-bearing veins in the world, outside of South Africa. The whole city was founded on mining, which is still its primary industry today.

As kids, we used to lie on our living room

floor and listen to the sound of the dynamite charges being exploded underground. There were miles upon miles of mine tunnels running under Timmins.

The explosions were created by the miners in their pursuit of the gold ore that snaked and turned endlessly in uneven patterns thousands of feet under the town.

From the outside, our lives looked picture perfect. We lived in a lovely house at the top of the hill on Murdock Street. My dad was a local town councilor and a successful businessman. We always had a nice car. My mother was very active within the community. Both my parents were devout Roman Catholics. We never missed Mass on Sundays. Yet, beneath this veneer of socioeconomic respectability, there was a terrifying existence being lived out in silence with my mother, brothers, sisters and myself.

We were the survivors of a violent, alcoholic home. The violence was both physical and emotional. From the time I was four years old, my father would bring out a 12-gauge shotgun in a drunken stupor and threaten our lives. At age 12, standing on a stairway in our lovely, middle-class Cape Cod home in Timmins, Ontario, my father loaded his 12-gauge, pumped it, aimed it at my mother and me, and then pulled the trigger.

The gun jammed, and he repeated the previous steps three more times. I can still hear the metallic click of the Winchester pump firing pin as he kept trying to get the gun to fire. It was our fault; he said in a drunken slur, that he had to do this. I was witnessing and experiencing insane behavior—which, to me, was normal.

I stood frozen in fear, paralyzed, unable to move. My life was dramatically altered at that moment. Never again would I have the innocence of childhood. It was ripped from me in those seconds.

Suddenly, my older brother Robert walked through the door. He charged up behind my dad, grabbed the gun and punched him so hard my father fell to the floor. He then bent down and grabbed my dad by the throat and started choking him, violently. My mother jumped on his back and started screaming, "You're going to kill him!"

It was the first time in his life my brother had ever raised a hand to my dad, but there were times when he was growing up that Dad had beaten him so hard with his belt that he had welts. My father would walk up to him and just flail him. My brother was so afraid he'd stand there and shake.

Well, this time, he was shaking from the top of his head to the tips of his shoes, but not from fear, from rage. My father lay on the floor, blood streaming out of his mouth, groaning. He held his ribs. He had hit his side on the telephone table as he fell from the punch my brother had given him. My brother just turned, looked at my mom and me, and walked out.

Shortly after, we moved away from that house and never returned. However, the damage done never left me until I relived the experience, and erased the consequences of it from my unconscious mind. Only then did I finally put my father to rest.

But before we did pick up and leave my father for good, there were incidents and events that contributed, in both a positive and negative way, to my future psychological and emotional development—believe me, I was not without responsibility for some them.

I attended St. John's Catholic School. It was a two-storey, two-room schoolhouse at the bottom of Empire Hill. From the first day of attending school, I didn't want to be there. I was filled with trepidation and discomfort. Early on, kids realized that if they raised their hands too quickly around me, I would jump—almost out of my skin.

I was precocious in an introverted sort of way. I was incapable of focusing on my schoolwork at a very young age. Undoubtedly, I had been suffering from what is known today as post-traumatic stress, although that term and the pathology of it was entirely unknown back then. I would have also been diagnosed with ADHD.

What I recall most about school are two things. First, that I felt I was stupid. Through my entire childhood, all I can ever remember hearing is I couldn't do anything right.

In fact, I have very few memories of my childhood—except for my closest friends. One incident stands out in my mind that had me realize, even at that young age, that I was blessed with an excellent sense of humor. We had the Grey Nuns as our teachers. I didn't want to go to school, and I'd stayed home on the second day of school without telling my mom. I just hid until she went to work at St. Mary's Hospital, and then went back in. I knew I'd have to go the next day, but I couldn't go that day. Sure enough, the next day I went, and Sister Mary Elizabeth—I think was her name—said, "David, where were you yesterday?"

Now, remember, I'm six. My mother is a nurse, and this woman is now towering over me, about seven feet tall in my mind, with a huge black strap, which she's slapping her hand in a very convincing way. My little brain has gone into overdrive looking for something, anything that's going to buy me time—when voila, a moment of genius. "I had to have an operation."

She was dumbfounded. Her eyes bulged as she stared in disbelief. "Show me where they operated," she said.

"Oh, I can't, Sister, it's private."

The other kids were laughing, which I liked.

So, as she's grabbing me by the ear and dragging me into the cloakroom, I'm thinking, this is not going well. Well, she is very upset with me, but here was a pattern that was to plague me a great deal of my life: not being honest when confronted with my behavior. She told me that she'd called my mother at the hospital inquiring where I was. My mom had no idea, but had come home and found me there and not said anything.

I'm standing in this cloakroom, Sister is upset, and I look up, and there is a flag with an elephant with big ears – it's black and green if I remember correctly, and I said, "What's that,

Sister?"

She was taken aback by my question. "It's Dumbo the Safety Elephant—it's to help you kids stay out of trouble."

I stared up at Dumbo, and out of my mouth came words that truly astounded me and proved to save my bacon that day. "Oh Dumbo, where are you now?" I said. Sister had to fight from breaking out laughing, and then she did something that astounded me. She slapped her hand and said, "If you ever tell anyone, I will indeed give you the strap. Go back in there and never lie to me again." That is the point where I got that charm pays off. I didn't understand it intellectually, but viscerally, I got it.

What is interesting to me today is that, while I felt I was stupid, I was interested in countless subjects and hobbies. I loved to read. I loved going to movies. I loved airplanes. I loved building and engineering.

For most kids, growing up in the mid to late 50s in Timmins was paradise. In the summer, the sun didn't set until late into the evening and rose very early. When I was eight or nine years old, I had to go to bed when it was still daylight out. I can still hear the songs of the robins and the cries of the nighthawks.

However, I could get up and get going by six in the morning. Conversely, in the winter, it was dark by four in the afternoon. The sun wouldn't rise until nearly eight in the morning.

My summers in Timmins were spent at Gillies Lake. I was safe at the lake. There was no screaming, no fighting, and no guns. I had my friends—Doug, Roy, Stan, Mark and Moe. We were like a little gang, albeit a very innocent one. We would swim from nine in the morning until late in the afternoon. I was often afraid or uncomfortable going home and I didn't know why back then.

My favorite pastime in the summer with my friends was to sleep in our backyard in a tent. I think it was in 1958 when the Russians launched Sputnik. We would just lie outside and watch it orbit the earth. It was incredible to think there was a dog up there that looked something like my dog Rex. The only difference was both of its back legs worked. One of Rex's legs had been severed on my grandparent's farm when he ran in front of the blades on the hay mower, and my grandfather couldn't stop the horses in time. That's how long ago it was. Real horsepower. So there was this dog, flying around the earth in a small garbage-can-sized capsule, and it ignited our imaginations.

The winters in Timmins were cold. I don't mean chilly; I mean cold. When you walked down the street in January, your winter boots crunched on the snow. Anyone who has ever lived in a cold climate knows the sound. In the winter, the cars all had chains on the rear tires to give them traction through the deep snow. The sound of the steel-chained tires rolling over the hard-packed snow, as they drove past our bedroom window at night, is a sound I'll never forget.

In the winter, we played hockey every day after school at the lake. I played Pee Wee for the Timmins Hotel Flyers. I remember one day when I was given the puck, and got so excited I turned around and scored on my unsuspecting goalie. From that episode, I inherited the name "Backward Brady." I was totally humiliated and embarrassed by that event. It was seared into my unconscious mind, and I thought I would never recover from it. That incident also dramatically affected my self-esteem, which was already subterranean from my home life and school, where I was a classic underachiever.

The other thing we loved to do in the winter was hanging on the back of the local buses and ski along on our winter boots. We used to hide at night behind parked cars, and when the bus came to a stop, we'd jump out and run and hang onto the big bumpers that used to stick out about six inches from the back of the bus. It was an unbelievable thrill to slide along at twenty and thirty miles an hour. In retrospect, it was incredibly dangerous. I would be terrified today if my kids did the same thing. But, to us, it was the way to get through the snow-covered streets of our town in the winter.

One night when I was around ten or eleven years old and my father was very drunk and angry; I remember sneaking out of the house and catching the bus as it headed down the hill. I was just going to go for a ride around the loop and head home. I just wanted to get out of the house. I was hanging on when I put my knee down on the snow. My snow pants had large leather patches that my mother had sewn on to strengthen them. Suddenly, a large boulder smashed into my kneecap, and I was in agony. I let go of the bus and tumbled off to the side of the road. I tried to stand and collapsed. I began dragging myself along the sidewalk, crying in pain. It took, at least, an hour to get home. My feet, face, and fingers were frostbitten when I arrived at the front door. I was in severe physical and emotional distress.

When I went into the house, my dad was passed out, and I just crawled upstairs to bed.

When my mother got home at midnight from the hospital, I was able to tell her what had happened. She was beside herself with worry, and she gave me a scolding I can still remember. Because of my father's alcoholism, my mother had taken a job as a nurse at St. Mary's Hospital to help pay the escalating bills my dad was acquiring because of his out-of-control drinking.

As a result, there was no one at home most nights, except my dad, who was always drunk. But it was that lack of supervision—the lack of attention to my well-being—that greatest of the issues that would plague me my whole life. I never learned to take care of myself properly.

No one supervised my homework, or even checked to see if I'd done any. My older sister would come home at midnight and find me sitting up watching television. I was ten years old. I was afraid to go to sleep.

At home, I found it impossible to focus. We were always waiting for my father's return with a sense of dread. We never knew if he would show up drunk or sober. I can still remember the time when he got sober and stayed sober for about three months. Our lives changed dramatically. That was the first time—in fact, the only time I remember ever doing anything with him. He took me fishing at Kamaskotia Lake. It was west of Timmins and took about an hour, in those days, to drive there on an old gravel road.

What's funny is I have a perfect memory of my dad taking me out and introducing me to a famous old prospector named Mr. Jameson. He lived alone all year round in a cabin by the lake. He had no electricity and no heat, except for a wood stove.

He was an interesting old man, full of incredible stories about the forest, bears, and hunting. I liked him. Going fishing with my dad was great. We just sat there, the two of us, in quiet contemplation. My father never really spoke to me, except when he was drunk. And then it didn't make sense.

I also remember the night my father came home drunk again. He was reeking of alcohol as he stumbled through the door. He was unsteady on his feet and hanging on to the doorjamb when he saw me. He leaned over and patted me on the head. I just felt sick inside, even though he handed me two dollars, which in 1958 would have been a fortune, so I could take my friends to the local corner store.

When my father was drunk, I had two paths of escape. In the summer, I could go down to my grandparent's Mc

Gale's farm near Cobalt, Ontario. Cobalt was the same town where my grandfather on my dad's side had founded his silver mine.

Part of the mythology of our family had been this breaking free of the Irish poverty on my grandfather's part, and there was a lake named after us in Cobalt, as well as the mine—Brady Cross Lake Silver Mines.

There was no money. But there were endless stories from my dad about how he would one day reclaim the family fortune by rediscovering a new vein—and getting the mine up and running again. I loved those stories. But they instilled in me a sense or hope of entitlement that one day I, too, could be counted among the wealthy, the wise, the cool, the hip that I yearned so much to be a part of as I grew up. I never really recognized at a young age just how insecure I was, or how I'd been dropped into the wrong family, the wrong town because I felt like an alien—and not one from this planet.

In Cobalt, I was able to roam around free as a bird. An old fence with a large gate that would swing out toward the main road surrounded the farm. When we arrived at the farm, I would jump out of my dad's car and run and open the gate.

I loved the farm. I enjoyed the peace and tranquility of it, even as a child. My father never stayed more than one night. For me, it was as close as I could get to a mythological Shangri-La.

I can still remember the smell of the wood stove and fresh bread baking in the morning. The house was constructed out of board and batten, which the weather had turned black, and was two stories high.

As a Canadian, we have a linguistic expression we add to the ends of our sentences. Most Americans and Europeans have a field day mimicking us. It's the big "eh," pronounced 'A'. Well, when I would say it, my grandmother would say B, C, and D, and so on, until I stopped.

There was an old, creaky stairway that led up to the second floor. The bedroom walls were rough cedar that had a lovely fragrance to it. There were old posters for various farm implements and automobiles from the 1930s and 40s tacked up on the walls. The chimney from the wood stove downstairs snaked its way through the different walls and rooms, and in winter was the primary source of heat. My grandmother had a 1911 record player that was sold by the T. Eaton Company of Canada out of their catalog.

It had a standing cabinet with a top you opened upward, exposing the record and a timeworn stylus that held a needle that had to be replaced every time you played one of the original discs. For power, you had to turn the side crank by hand. She loved it, and I still have it today.

My grandfather grew potatoes and hay as his principal crops. He also had several horses, as well as quite a few cows and pigs.

Years before, he'd run a dairy and a lumberyard, and all the equipment was still in place. It was there I learned to love the smell of a barn: the mingling of manure and hay represents one of the most comforting smells I know. I think that's is why today, I have a house in the country across from a working farm. Across from the barn and just north of the house was my grandfather's machine shop. It, too, was an olfactory smorgasbord: the smell of oil, grease and gasoline mixed with old cedar walls and shakes. The ground was covered with clover that used to stick to the cuff of your pants. I could rub my fingers over my pant cuffs and smell it for weeks after I'd gotten back home.

We drew water from an outdoor spring that was as pure and clean as water could be. It was also incredibly cold, and it always ran, in the heat of summer or the freezing temperatures of winter.

There was an old school on the property. It was fully equipped in the 1950s, although not in use. I could not get the story straight as to who owned it or built it, but my recollection is that my granddad had made it in the early part of the 20th century to educate his kids.

It had desks, blackboards and a large hand bell that was great to ring. I would spend hours there playing school by myself. I was blessed with a great imagination, which began to expand exponentially with all of the tools of pedagogy that were present and long forgotten in that classroom.

One of the other main attractions for me at the farm was a stream that ran through the property. I discovered it when I was about six or seven years of age From then until I was about eleven years old, I would take my grandmother's washtub and float down the stream. I had great fun, and it was there that my ongoing fascination with Tom Sawyer and Huckleberry Finn would emerge. It was at the farm that my love of reading began to develop. And it was those two books along with the Hardy Boy's Series that began my journey into the world of my imagination. I was able to paint a vast mental panorama and experience emotional and visceral reaction in my mind's eye.

My grandfather was a very quiet man. He would often take me to town in his old 1940s International truck. I loved that truck and going for rides in it with him.

When I couldn't get away to the farm, my other escape from my father was an imaginary world up in my room.

Our bedroom had a bunk bed, where my two older brothers slept. I had a little bed next to a small cupboard on the opposite side of the room. The walls were a peaceful green.

Whenever it got too noisy, or there was too much screaming or violence, I would take my pillow and crawl into that cupboard. I originally thought it must have been a fairly big closet until I went up to Timmins to revisit the house with my former wife, Deb, and our two children, Brendan and Laurel. It was part of my journey to try and put my past behind me and lay the ghosts to rest that haunted my subconscious or unconscious mind for all those years. At that point, I was in my early 40s, and we'd left when I was 13 – so nearly thirty years had passed.

My river meandered slowly through mango trees and weeping willows, and lush vegetation covered each shore. I could hear the sound of the cicadas in the branches of the trees. I would lie on my back and imagine the sun reflecting off the canopy of translucent green leaves overhead as we slowly floated down the river – regardless of whether it was summer or winter. While growing up in Timmins, the Deep South of the United States seemed appealing – especially in winter, when we were walking to school in 20 below zero weather.

I can also remember crying. I cried so hard and so long that I felt like I was going to die. I believe at one of these occasions a pillow was put over my face to stop me. I can still remember the sensation of smothering. To this day, I cannot have anything near my face, or I go into a horrible panic. What sticks vividly in my memory is thinking, "Am I normal? Is this normal? Do other kids feel like me? Am I going insane? Am I going to die?"

I always felt like I was going to die as a child.

As I got older, my sisters and brothers began leaving home once they were old enough. First, my oldest sister left to go to boarding school when she was fourteen or fifteen. Then, my oldest brother Robert got married when I was about eleven or twelve. My sister Liz moved to Toronto, and then there was just my one older brother, Jim, and I at home.

I failed grade six in Timmins, the year my dad had tried to murder my mother and I. What sticks in my memory so is the shame I felt. I was twelve years old, and I had already survived, according to one therapist, the same emotional and physical violence that many people do in war zones. I had tried to explain to one of my teachers about our home life, and he wouldn't believe me, as he "knew' my father – and in his opinion, my dad was a great guy.

But, it was on August 1, 1960, shortly after the incident with the shotgun that my father, sober, loaded our luggage, and my mother and me in his Buick and started the long drive to Toronto. I have no memory whatsoever of the trip, which took over ten hours. I don't remember him ever saying he was sorry for what happened that day in the house. I can only remember seeing my first four-lane highway, the 400, and weeping willows. Like most of my childhood, it is a blank. When he dropped us off at my sister's at the top of Avenue Road Hill, I have no recollection of him leaving, although I'm sure he said goodbye. I just don't remember.

Growing up in our home exposed us to a lot of unhealthy messages. My father believed that you were nothing if you weren't financially successful. The irony is that he was always in debt and overspending. When drunk, he would go on about how much money we were going to have when he got the mine up and running again. I never tired of his optimism. It is the one gift he gave me: My sense of optimism about the future, no matter how far down I am.

My father's alcoholism robbed him of his solvency – as best we can figure it out. As it would turn out, alcoholism was to rob my dad of a lot more than material wealth.

It cost him everything: his family, his self-respect, and his standing in the community. The paradox was that he was so well thought of by so many people. As I mentioned earlier, he was a town councilor. I've often wondered what went through his mind as he lay dying alone, and only my one sister and my mother went to visit him. That must have been horrible for him. But it does bring home the point, "You reap what you sow."

I recently received an email from someone I'd known as a ten-year-old, and he referred to my dad as a real gentleman. A man, who would help solve disputes in taverns and barrooms, but was a homicidal maniac at home. My father was a great guy, if you weren't related to him. He treated strangers like family and family like strangers. I am able to recognize today how sick my father was. I can imagine how he felt, as well. I felt just like him near the end of my own addictions—beaten and in emotional agony. I honestly don't know why he was never able to stop drinking. I don't know why I was given the gift of sobriety so many years ago, and not him.

As a young man, however, the message that without material wealth, without success, you are a nobody, would hound me for the next thirty years. I was driven to succeed, to be someone of prominence. It would influence whom I liked, where I lived and what I wanted out of life. Never once did I think about what might make me happy. The drive was for success and material wealth.

4. SUMMER IN THE CITY

We arrived at my sister's apartment at 394 Avenue Road across from De La Salle Oakland's, the private Catholic School my mother had arranged for me to attend. They had also agreed to allow me to move on to the next grade. It was an impressive school, built on the crest of the Avenue Road hill, overlooking downtown Toronto. The Christian Brothers who ran and taught at the school lived in a beautiful old Victorian mansion on the property. The school itself was the exemplary early1950s architecture. Structural functionalism.

I liked De La Salle a lot. I loved the drum corps, which in my mind was the real reason I wanted to go there. At that time, I wanted to play the drums more than anything else—but at first, I found it difficult to adjust from a small northern Ontario mining town to a large urban center.

I can still remember my first day walking down Avenue Road hill. There were six lanes of traffic. The first thing that baffled me was why anyone would call a street "Avenue Road." I always thought it was one or the other. It was astounding to me that there could be that many cars.

That August, the air was hot and humid and hung like a blanket over the city. A strange odor intrigued me. Not a bad smell, just a smell that was unique. I soon came to the conclusion that this smell was a trace of chlorine coming from a large swimming pool, just north of us in Eglington Park. I began going there every day, but meeting kids proved to be harder than in Timmins.

As I wandered around the neighborhood, I was enthralled by the various sights and sounds; English sports cars, which proliferated the streets of this young urban city where everywhere. I loved all the MGs, Austin Healey's and Triumph TR3s. My neck strained as I glanced up at 500 Avenue Road, this beautiful gray and white modern apartment building at the top of the hill, north of St. Clair. I would end up living across the street from it for several years.

I can still remember standing in wonder at

the sight of my first streetcar.   The Red Rocket, as they were referred to, mesmerized me.

These new experiences of city life, made me feel so sophisticated.   I went into a store and picked up my first cardboard carton of milk.   No bottle.

And then, I strolled east along St. Clair toward Yonge Street and came to what was to become one of my major haunts growing up. Fran's Restaurant.

I'd never seen anything like it.   It had square glass windows across the front section, where there were booths and several huge plate-glass windows in a semi-circle on the west side overlooking the dining room.   There was a large neon sign with Fran's written in green, and light bulbs always blinking in sequence around the perimeter of it.

Every day after school at Del, I would head over to Fran's Restaurant.   We always had the same thing: chips and a cherry Coke, or a toasted Danish and a cherry Coke.   All of the kids from our neighborhood use to congregate there when they weren't hanging out at the old Granite Club. There were boys from Upper Canada College and De La Salle, and the girls from Bishop Strachan, Havergal and Branksome Hall.   There were also the kids from the public schools: Brown School, Deer Park and North Toronto.

There was a hierarchy. Those from high school sat in the booths, while the grade-seven and eight's, with whom I started out, had to sit on the stools, and then later on in the back.

The back was built when we turned fifteen and sixteen. Old Fran thought it would be easier for him and his staff if they stuck us in a small room, which he later converted into a cocktail bar, to keep our antics from disturbing the other paying (and mature) customers, who found our behavior upsetting.

In retrospect, what amazes me was the range of interesting people who used to congregate at Fran's Restaurant.

On any given night, you would see actors like the renowned Canadian comedy team of Wayne and Schuster. Their appearances on the Ed Sullivan Show in the 1960s made them famous. Another local resident was the remarkable Glenn Gould. It seems that he ate at Fran's every night. But none of us had a clue who he was or what he was doing. His apartment was less than a block away, on St. Clair Avenue West.

Old Fran Deck, the owner, used to see us

outside and offer us coupons that entitled us to free apple pie. He understood marketing and loyalty.

Those half a dozen apple pies over five years brought him a return of forty-one years of commitment, because I went to Fran's up until 2001, when it finally closed down. When I lived in Vancouver, Los Angeles, New York or moved back to Toronto, whenever I was back in the city, I always went back to Fran's. People could never understand my fondness for it, especially as it was beginning to wear on the edges.

When I got into the De La Salle Drum Corps, I was down in the St. Clair Ravine, practicing my drums. By then, we had moved from Avenue Road to another apartment at One Heath Street East.

My mother continued to look for a house we could live in near my school. But because we were living in an apartment, the ravine was the only place I could go to practice my drums.

From the dead end at Heath Street East, there was a set of wooden stairs that led down the ravine to the river at the bottom of it. One of the great things Toronto's early planners did was set aside so many natural forests and parks for their citizens to enjoy. There was an occasional table set up where you could have a picnic lunch. The path was lined with felled trees and brush. In the spring and summer, I still remember the gorgeous smell of all the natural flowers and leaves as they began to bloom.

The whole park system was set up with walking paths and resting spots where you could sit and watch birds, or listen to the river running through rapids at certain locations. During the day, there was no one there. It was like my private forest – in truth, it reminded me of my old home in Northern Ontario. It was a natural oasis in the middle of the city. I would either stand by the table or sit on it and practice my paradiddles, flamadiddles or drum rolls.

One day, as I was practicing my drums, a young fellow my age appeared and said his father wanted to speak to me. His name was Rick Taylor. He had another friend visiting him by the name of John Brower. Rick and his parents lived in a large house where Heath Street East ended at the ravine, where I had decided to practice.

Rick's father, a very suave and sophisticated gentleman, asked me if this was the only place where I could practice. I told him I didn't have anywhere else to go, and he conceded, "All right, then."

My meeting John Brower, however, was to begin the longest-running friendship I've ever had in my life. It is still going strong, fifty-odd years later.

What I liked about John then was that he lived in an apartment, too. He and I were the only two teenagers in our neighborhood I knew whose parents were either separated or divorced. He was very cool compared to me. He'd grown up sophisticated. His dad was a lawyer. His uncle and godfather was one of Canada's prime ministers. He had two sisters, Linda and Debbie who were nice. I used to spend a lot of time at his apartment, and John got me interested in music. He loved music.

He introduced me to R&B, and we would head downtown to the Toronto nightspots every weekend to listen to all the great bands that were around at that time.

Ronnie Hawkins and the Hawks had Robbie Robertson and Levon Helm in the band. This group went on to play backup for Bob Dylan and then went on to become The Band.

, a few years ago I completed a remarkable series entitled Yonge Street, Toronto Rock & Roll Stories that featured John, as well as almost everyone we saw back then. From Ronnie

Hawkins and Robbie Robertson from to all the great musicians I'd been a fan of, including John Kay from Steppenwolf and David Clayton Thomas of Blood Sweat and Tears.

Fifty years later, I still remember holding my first party at the apartment on Heath Street East—or rather, the horror of it. I was afraid that no one would show up, that no one would enjoy himself or herself, that people would think we were hicks because we lived in an apartment and they all had beautiful homes in our neighborhood. I was so ashamed we had to live in an apartment after our beautiful house in Timmins. As it turned out, everyone had a great time. They couldn't have cared less where I lived. I was the only one consumed by those feelings of insecurity and inferiority, but they were very real to me. Low self-esteem is one of the hallmarks of those of us who come from dysfunctional or trauma based families.

Then came another black period for me. Two years after we arrived in Toronto, my mother came down with breast cancer. It was 1962. I was informed she had to go in for extensive surgery and recuperation.

It was decided that I should go to boarding school in North Bay. I didn't know how I felt about that. By then, I'd stopped missing Timmins, and I was fairly well ensconced in Toronto.

Though I didn't feel like moving again, I wasn't doing very well in school. Going to boarding school felt like moving to me.

However, at that point, I had never learned the basics of studying, and because of the insanity while growing up in the house with my dad, I was hopelessly behind in all the fundamentals. It was felt that the priests and the structured environment would help me get back on track.

I spent two years at Scollard Hall in North Bay. North Bay is on the shores of Lake Nipissing in Northern Ontario. It was built along the Canadian Shield, the granite outcroppings that form the backbone of the Province of Ontario.

It was also home to NORAD and the ICBM ballistic missile silos. It was not a great place to be in October 1962 when the Cuban Missile Crisis erupted. North Bay, the missile silos and the military air base that had a large United States military contingent were one of the USSR's primary targets.

I can remember the priests telling us that if

we heard the alarm, the air raid siren, we were to crawl under our desks or run down to the basement.

I knew lying under a desk was going to do about as much good as putting up your arm to stop a speeding car from running you down. We were glued to the radio every night as the events unfolded. We all talked about dying. I was particularly quiet on the subject. It was incredible to have lived through that period and realize that we, as a culture, came so close to annihilating ourselves from the face of the earth over pride and ego.

I remember feeling very alone. Isolated. I made a few friends that I stuck close to, and I was riddled with insecurity. I was not doing too well in school, just getting by.

I remember meeting this tremendously good-looking girl, Sally Ann Ward when I was 15. Sally was the highlight of that school year. I felt like a star at our school prom. God, it felt great to be liked! It was an entirely innocent relationship – I never did more than kiss her good night. But it was the biggest kiss of my life. I know that my standing went way up in that school when I captured Sally's heart. She was stunningly beautiful, and about two inches taller than me. God does have a good sense of humor and does come to the rescue when we need it most. I've often wondered whatever happened to her.

The other significant event that unfolded at Scollard Hall was the onset of Beatlemania. What happened was that someone brought me a copy of the Beatles' first album. I had the same haircut as they did, and I immediately fell in love with their music. I would listen to it all night on my transistor radio.

The first night I ever really got drunk was the weekend after Father Fedy called me in, sat me down and said, "We have bad news. It appears your mother is not doing too well, and she may not live. We have to figure out what to do with you. Are you all right with going home to your father?" I was terrified at this prospect.

Father Fedy was incredibly kind but tough. I just sat there in a state of shock. Years before, when my dad had hurt me so much, I'd made a promise to myself that I would never cry again, and I couldn't cry then. I just walked out of his office in a state of numbness and went back to my room. When my roommate asked me what was going on, I said nothing. I didn't know how to open up to anyone. My mother and John Brower were the only two people I'd ever told how I felt.

Years later, I was to realize that I couldn't feel emotions other than rage, lust, fear, and jealousy. That was it. I wouldn't have known an emotion if it had come up and hit me with a two-by-four. At that moment, though, I was overwhelmed with fear. I was frozen emotionally.

I fired a note down to John and told him I was in trouble. I couldn't express myself very well at the time. He misunderstood and sent me back a pack of pornographic pictures, which he thought was going to help me. On the envelope, he'd put: Don't open, personal, for Dave Brady only. Well, the priests opened them up, and the next thing you know, I'm up getting the cane. I'm thinking, "What the hell! I didn't even see the pictures, and I'm getting it." I glanced over as Father whacked me, but I couldn't steal a peek. Sometimes there's no justice. God's sense of humor again.

The principal of Upper Canada College, John's school, was notified, and we both got in trouble. That weekend a couple of my schoolmates decided we should go out and rent a cheap hotel room and buy some alcohol. This would be my first drink, which would be a drunk, which would set up my pattern for drinking. I never, to the best of my knowledge, ever had a social drink. I drank because I liked the effect of it.

After we'd acquired the room, we went out to the liquor store and attempted to get several individuals to buy us a bottle. No one would. Finally, a real poor-looking man came by, and we enticed him by saying we'd buy him a bottle too. He was off like a rocket to get our liquor, and then back in a flash with the goods. We went to our room. We had a case of twenty-four beers and a bottle of lemon gin.

I can still remember the smell of the lemon gin to this day – it was awful. I never threw up so hard in my life. But something happened to me that night. All the fears, all the insecurities, all the doubts I had disappeared, and I felt what I assumed normal must have felt like for the first time in my life.

The problem was I had all the symptoms of a chronic alcoholic from my first drink. I blacked out within minutes of taking it. In other words, I was conscious, talking to everyone, having a blast, but I had no recollection whatsoever. I threw up, passed out and when I came to, I thought, "Wow! I can't wait to do that again." From that moment on, I drank to change the way

I felt and to stop the constant fear. It gave me a very temporary relief from all the feelings of insecurity, anxiety and self-consciousness that had plagued me my entire life.

As it turned out, I also became incredibly obnoxious. Scollard Hall was not working out. I couldn't concentrate. I was worried sick about my mother, and I couldn't stand living that far away from her. I called my brother Jim, who came and helped me sneak away one spring morning. I hadn't yet completed grade 10 and was headed back to Toronto, but I wanted to get home and see my mom.

5. HOME AGAIN

On my return to Toronto, my mother shocked everyone with a miraculous recovery. She enrolled me in a very exclusive private school, Cantab College, in Forest Hill. My schoolmates included George Eaton, whose family controlled the largest retailing empire in the British Commonwealth, and John Barron, whose family was extremely successful.

George lived on Dunvegan Road in Forest Hill. To enter his house you had to pass by a security guard John, who seemed always to be on duty whenever I was there.

John Barron lived on Rosedale Heights Drive. He always dressed impeccably. White button-down shirts, black slacks and black loafers. That was his look. He smoked Export cigarettes with no filters and kept his change in his back pocket. I have no idea of why that impressed me, but it did.

At that age, all that mattered were cars and

girls. I remember when John Barron got his Sunbeam Tiger. It was an English sports car with a Ford V-8. He fitted it with dual Abarth exhausts. It sounded like no other car I'd ever heard.

A deep, throaty growl. He would put his foot on the gas, and the Tiger would simply sit there, wheels spinning, with smoke pouring off the pavement. We would go cruising most days after school. He too was a friend of John Brower.

Whenever I compared myself to people like George Eaton or John Barron, I was filled with embarrassment because my mother had to work at Sick Kids as a nurse while their families were so wealthy. One evening at George's home, I was going on about my dad when George quietly leaned over and said, "It doesn't matter what your father does. That's not why you're here."

It shocked me at first, but in his way, he was saying, "Look, shut up. Nothing you say will impress us. We don't talk about who we are, neither should you."

Only I believe he did it with compassion. From that moment on, I had a great deal of respect for George. He was, in my opinion, a very misunderstood and underrated human being. He had incredible insight and wisdom for his age.

When he raced cars, the press referred to him as the world's richest hippie. I believe he was doing it to prove to himself that he had the ability, and not just family wealth.

I introduced him to John Brower, and he and his brother Thor became partners in the first big rock concerts that took place in Toronto that John produced.

A few years later, George was involved with John in bringing John Lennon to Toronto. One could argue that the Toronto Rock & Roll Revival was the cause of the breakup of the Beatles. It was the first time John Lennon ever played without the Beatles when he appeared with Eric Clapton, Klaus Voorman, and Yoko Ono on stage at Varsity Arena in the fall of 1969. It's believed that it was on Lennon's return from this concert that he told the other Beatles it was over.

However, a few years before that event, sitting in George's house one night, watching one of the first color televisions I'd ever seen, we saw a show that had a new Pontiac GTO. Within weeks, it seemed, George had one. Black with black interior. It had a 389 cubic inch engine with three two-barrel carburetors and four on the floor. The power it had was outrageous.

He took several of us out one night and

drove around a traffic circle in Forest Hill so fast I thought we would crash. I lay in the back screaming, terrified because, years before, my father, drunk, had taken me in his car and we had piled up. Then my face had hit the dashboard. I was always afraid of cars, but it was also exhilarating beyond anything I had ever done. I alternated between laughing hard and screaming even louder. It was great fun!

That summer, I met Beverly Willoughby at Fran's. I was sixteen, and she was fourteen and going to Branksome Hall. I was so shy; I could hardly get up the courage to speak to her. It turned out there was competition for her affections. I had to fight a "grease ball" in our neighborhood on the mean streets of Deer Park at Yonge and St. Clair. (Those who live in the city will get the humor of that. It's like saying the means streets of Beverly Hills or midtown Manhattan. Not too mean at all.)

I bought my first car from this fellow—a 1953 Studebaker. It had no brakes, and I drove right into the garage door of his apartment building. He said all it needed was a little brake fluid, and I would just have to pump the brakes a few times. It did, I did, and off I went. In retrospect, I could have easily gotten myself or someone else killed.

On one occasion, my arch-nemesis was sitting with Bev at Fran's. I walked in, and he could clearly see I was upset. He got up, walked over and said, "Get lost. She's mine."

Naturally, I challenged him; only to find out he was one of the local tough guys. Having grown up with my older brother, who beat the crap out of me on a regular basis, I didn't think this fight could be any different.

But with my brother, I didn't figure he'd try to hurt me. This guy, he wanted to hurt me—bad. We stood on St. Clair, with me provoking him. Finally, when I figured he was going to punch my lights out, I kicked him straight in the testicles. He just stood there, the color draining from his face, and then he let out a blood-curdling scream and came at me. I took my high school steel-edged binder and drilled him as hard as I could across the face. Blood gushed out of his mouth and started pouring profusely down the front of his clothes, but he just got angrier. At that moment the thought was born: "Better to run today, and live to fight another day." This guy was not going down—but I was if I stayed another second. I took off, and he never caught me.

I was concerned that he would try and get back at me for the next several weeks; yet, while he lived in the neighborhood, I never saw him again. What had come out of me at that moment was a lot of unexpressed rage. I had hurt him when my fight-or-flight reflexes had kicked in automatically, and in retrospect, I suspect my anger may have frightened him as much as it did me.

Beverly was not too impressed with my actions, but I was bound and determined to go out with her. John Brower found out she was having a party at her parents' home in Rosedale, and we made plans to crash it.

It was one of the first times I resorted to drinking to get up the nerve to meet someone, and it set up a pattern for me at that young age.

I'm grateful to say I didn't make a scene at her home that night. I met her mom and dad, both of whom were friendly and warm. Within a year of meeting Bev, her mother came down with terminal cancer, and I was at their home the night she died. I believe Bev was only fifteen years old when her mom passed away. Her mother was a remarkably kind woman. Her dad was a very special person, too. I came to view him as the father I never had and always wished I could have.

Thank God for John Brower's grandmother

that summer. She would lend John her Studebaker Grand Turismo, the car John had convinced her to buy, for weeks at a time. What a great car for an 80-year-old grandmother to be driving. It was a two-door hardtop with bucket seats and one of the first curved dashes I'd ever seen, a tachometer, and a great V-8. It was one of the best production grand touring automobiles ever made.

We would get dressed up in our Madras or Gant button-down white or oxford-blue shirts, our beige pants and our Bass Weejun penny loafers and go cruising. At this point, we were praying to get lucky, but generally, we had no luck at all.

Some our friends had cottages in Muskoka. To those uninitiated, the Muskokas are arguably one of the most beautiful geographical regions of Canada outside of British Columbia or the Rockies's in Alberta. To get there, you travel two to three hours north from Toronto. Made famous by several of the Group of Seven, Canada's renowned artists from the early part of the twentieth century, the Muskokas contain pristine lakes and stunning evergreen forests.

Over the years, celebrities from all over the world have come to enjoy the stunning beauty of the lakes. Who can blame them? The fragrance of the fresh pine trees and the sound of the wind rustling through the leaves of the poplar trees were hypnotic. I loved the quiet, the gorgeous shoreline along Lake Joseph, the smell of cedar logs in the big fireplaces that burned brightly when the air got cool and crisp, and the call of loons on the lake at night. It is one of the most beautiful sounds in all of nature. There's magic to Muskoka.

Each cottage was bigger and more luxurious than the next. They were truly spectacular. In the mid-sixties, Bala and Port Carling were the greatest places on earth to be, if you were a teenager—except for the beaches of California, which I would get to in 1967.

The downside for me to being there in the summer was that I couldn't understand why we had to be poor when I compared myself to the kids I knew, whose parents were captains of industry or cabinet ministers in the governing political party of the day. I wanted to live in a mansion. I wanted money more than anything else in life. I wanted to be somebody because I believed it was the only way I was ever going to feel all right about myself. How wrong I was!

In Toronto, Yorkville Village was starting to

happen in the early sixties. John Brower and I would head down every Friday and Saturday night to the different clubs. We would sit and listen to John Kay's band, The Sparrows, which was to become Steppenwolf—whose big hit, God Damn the Pusher Man, was written by the late Hoyt Axton. Hoyt would star in Dixie Lanes for me twenty years later. A friend of John Brower's by the name of John Godesby played in the band. He became Goldie McJohn. We would also go down to the L'Coq Dor and listen to Ronnie Hawkins and the Hawks.

When I look back at myself back then, I have no idea why I was so insecure about my looks. I was so hard on myself. I was a good-looking kid, but I thought I was physically ugly. I was stunned anytime a pretty young woman agreed to go out with me as my self-esteem was so low.

It was here that my drinking started to get out of control. John and I used to hang out at the Embassy Tavern in the Wild Night Room, where draft beer was fifteen cents a glass. On the weekends, they would bring in Fats Domino, Roy Orbinson, or other comparable acts to the Palm Grove Lounge downstairs. I can remember the first time the waiter, Garnett, allowed me to sit down and drink. He looked at me and, with his rapier-like humor, said, "Christ, are you even old enough to drive?" I was, but that was it.

From our private school, we would head down for lunch, and I would come back to school too loaded to do any work.

The second hangout I frequented was the Place Pigalle on Avenue Road. It was more hip, with more university students. But I was 18 years old at this point.

My friends and I would go to the Place or the Embassy on a regular basis and watch old WC Fields movies at the University of Toronto. I loved WC. I particularly loved his take on being an alcoholic and his references to Godfrey Daniels— his way of saying goddammit, which the censors would never let him do. To me, Mae West was the epitome of an independent woman. I loved her style and humor. Those were carefree days, filled with fun and partying.

My passion at that point was fast motorcycles and cars. I loved British bikes. When George Eaton got his GTO, I went to my mother, and I said, "If you don't get me a motorcycle, I'm going to kill myself."

I couldn't cope with the peer pressure. My mother arranged for me to see a psychiatrist.

After an hour, he brought my mom in and said, "I'd buy him a motorcycle."

Mine wasn't a cry for help. It was an acceptance that I couldn't stand the way I was feeling, and death looked preferable to me at that stage of my life. It was just so embarrassing to be poor—having no money, but being around these kids whose families were extremely wealthy.

My mother finally acquiesced, and I was able to get a motorcycle. A 1958 BSA 650. In those days, that was quite a bike. In retrospect, it was odd to see me in my private school uniform, so skinny, pushing this unbelievably fast bike down the street to get it started. I had changed the pistons, so the compression was too high for me to kick it over.

Once I had tried to kick it when the timing was too retarded, and it backfired and hurled me over the handlebars. I wasn't about to do that again anytime soon. So, I would run down the street, jump on and put it in second gear, and away I would go. I loved the freedom of a motorcycle. I loved the speed. I loved standing out—being different. It felt good.

I have no idea how I survived on that motorcycle. Most nights I drove it drunk. My worst motorcycle accident occurred one night when I came up Avenue Road hill, flat out in fourth gear, pushing well over one hundred and sixty kilometers (a hundred miles) an hour. I had no helmet.

As I came across the streetcar tracks at St. Clair, a Toronto City Roads truck was ahead, wetting down the road at Heath Street to clean it. I was too drunk to notice, and as I looked up and saw the water truck, I started to try frantically to gear down. Suddenly, my back wheels began to break out on me because of the wet road, and I had to gear up again. As I banked right into the long S turn around Upper Canada College, the bike just went out from underneath me. I can remember thinking, "This is going to hurt."

I let go of the handlebars and tried to jump off. It was too late. Everything started to go in slow motion. I saw the fence coming at me, and I could see the bike heading toward the wall. The trouble was, I was starting to pass the bike in midair. I don't know what happened next. I just remember hitting the wall and everything going blank and then coming to with cars stopped, and people running over to look at me.

The only thing I can imagine is that I was so drunk that I completely relaxed when I crashed, and, as a result, wasn't killed. The clutch handle had pierced the side of my finger, and I still have the scar today.

The knee, which I had hit as a kid, was smashed in, but I managed to stand up. When I convinced the people who had stopped that I was okay, they left, and I crawled down Lonsdale to my house. Later, I was awakened by the sound of the police banging at our front door, but by then I was sober, and they didn't charge me with drunk driving. I explained I was in so much pain that I'd passed out. They believed me because it was true.

My most traumatic car accident happened around the same time. We were at our friend's house, partying across from Casa Loma. We were all drinking. When we left the party, we ended up on Dunvegan Road in Forest Hill.

I was without a date, and a little bored as I remember it, so I decided to liven things up and walk out onto the street. There was a large pile of leaves at the side of the road. I decided to light them on fire. My friend, who was driving, saw what I was doing and instructed me to get back in the car.

I jumped in, and we peeled away, heading north and then west over to Spadina. We were going quite fast along Spadina Road when he decided to make an abrupt left turn, and we crashed into a tree. There was blood everywhere.

The young woman in the front had smashed her face, and the girl beside me had fluid coming out of her ears—brain fluid. She was in very serious condition. I was able to get out of the car, and I ran to a house and started pounding on a door. Within minutes, the police and ambulances were there. The police questioned us all, but I don't know what the outcome was.

In later years as I started to think about it, I always wondered why I didn't die or get seriously injured in one of those accidents. A mystery. We were all left scarred from that evening: some of us emotionally, some physically.

But those times were not all bad, and there were times of just plain, ordinary fun. The highlight of my teenage years was the day John Brower, and I were driving our motorcycles down Avenue Road, just north of Upper Canada College.

There was a black limousine with a police escort ahead of us. It pulled into the school grounds. We decided to follow it and see who it was. The driver headed around the back of the school, and then pulled up in front of the main building, just in front of the old clock tower facing Avenue Road—and to my shock, four young men crawled out: John, Paul, George, and Ringo.

They were changing cars so they could sneak into the King Edward Hotel. I was so stunned; all I could do was stand there. John Brower sauntered up to John Lennon and simply introduced himself, and said, "We're going to work together."

Lennon smiled and laughed. As I indicated earlier, four years later, John produced the Toronto Rock and Roll Revival with John Lennon and the Plastic Ono Band.

When John Brower decided to move to Los Angeles to go to school (and follow his girlfriend from Toronto there), I felt as if I had lost a part of myself. John would call me and describe what was happening—the weather, the cars, the girls. I wanted to get to LA more than anything on earth. Finally, after about eighteen months, he returned to Toronto.

It was at this point that I decided I didn't want to waste my life screwing up in Toronto. Like me, John Brower was committed to succeeding.

We were two young teenagers with

something to prove. We both knew the only chances we were ever going to get were the ones we created, especially among the kids we hung out with, in our neighborhood.

I remember the day he had me over to his mom's when he first returned from LA in the spring of 1967. He pulled out a forty-five record of this unknown band. He'd heard them at a club a few weeks before in LA. The song was Light My Fire, and the band was The Doors. I can remember thinking, "Wow! Is this ever good!" He looked at me and asked the question I was to ask many others: "Are you in? We can have our record company."

Brower, Brady & Chueba Productions was born. I went to Bev's dad and outlined my plan to him, and asked him if he would finance us. He agreed, and six weeks later, we were off to LA. We had a friend from high school who had a phenomenal voice and a great talent as a songwriter. His name was Bob McBride. John and I signed him to a management contract and jumped on an American Airlines flight to Los Angeles with him.

6. CALIFORNIA DREAMING

In the summer of 1967, the Sunset Strip was heaven if you were under thirty. It was American Graffiti turned upside down. Gone were the hot rods, and in were Porsches. Gone were preppy slacks, and in were bell-bottom pants with flowers. Gone was the neatly cropped and styled short hair. Our locks flowed long.

Sunset Strip was beyond anything a twenty-year-old from Toronto could have imagined. It was like having twenty Yorkville Villages. We strolled past Pandora's Box, the Whiskey, Ben Franks (now Mel's on Sunset) just west of The Source, the first health food restaurant I'd ever seen, which was made famous in Woody Allen's film Manhattan.

At that point, John had developed an oldie

album business with one of the legends of LA radio, Dick Hug, or Huggy Boy. His cohort on Big XERB out of Tijuana Mexico was Wolf Man Jack. This was long before Wolf Man's prominence in the mid- to late-70s on television. This was in the days of "Get your Wolf Man roach holder, baby." Anyone who knew his voice will remember that refrain.

We moved into a mid-range motel/residence called the Hollywood Hawaiian. It was a typical late 40s or early 50s motel apartment located at the corners of Yucca and Grace, right in Hollywood. The manager was an odd fellow with large bumps protruding from his cranium. Bob McBride anointed him 'Knobby,' a name that unfortunately followed him all the months we were there.

Every week Knobby would be pounding on our door, looking for the next week's rent. In advance! Musicians! They don't have the best reputations. The motel had a pool with rooms built around it. The air was fragrant with the smell of plants, juxtaposed against the yellow hanging smog. On some days, it was so thick you couldn't see the hood of your car. In spite of that, summer in LA was gorgeous. Everything was green, and beautiful flowers bloomed everywhere.

As it turned out, the Hollywood Hawaiian was full of great musicians. Charles Lloyd was staying there. There was a young woman who kept playing beautifully, but one morning, I was so hung over I told her that if she couldn't sing any better than that, she should think about a second career. She slammed the door in my face and told me to "drop dead." She went on to sell millions and millions of albums. This was the first time in my life when I opened my mouth to change feet—in a major way.

The whole time I was riddled with an abnormal fear. It was with me from the time I woke up until I went to bed unless I medicated myself with alcohol.

We had brought Bob McBride down from Toronto to get him a record deal. By sheer determination, we got in to see Doovid Barskin at Capitol Records, as well as A&M Records, Herb Alpert's new label. He was just beginning to be a major player. We also managed to get Bob and ourselves on the old Joe Pyne talk show.

Normally Joe Pyne loved to tear people apart. It turned out he had either been from Montreal or loved Montreal because he was just great to us.

Bob had a tremendous voice. His singing

and songwriting talent was remarkable. After his contract with us, he went on to be the lead singer for the Canadian rock band Lighthouse. He sang all of their number one tunes: One Fine Morning, Sunny Days, etc. But in those days, Bob was out of control emotionally. He couldn't stop telephoning his girlfriend back in Toronto. Long-distance phone calls in 1967 were not cheap. He ended up running up close to eight hundred dollars on the hotel bill. To me, that was a fortune. I got incredibly angry at him, and it was the only time I remember that we ever came to a screaming match. I may have bonked him on the head with a whiskey bottle, but I'm not sure if that happened. It's stuck in the recesses of my unconscious.

Most of our time was spent at the Whisky A Go Go. On any given night, you could go in and see bands like The Righteous Brothers, The Byrds, or our heroes, The Doors. That was incredible. One night, I met Mama Cass when she was visiting someone at our motel. She was an extremely nice woman. I remember being so impressed by just how genuine and affable she seemed.

John married Michelle Finney, the young star of Razzle Dazzle, whose show on CBC was a tremendous hit in Canada. Her parents had taken her to LA to expand her career. One evening, Michelle introduced me to a very pretty teenage girl. As we talked, I found out her dad was Howie Horowitz. He produced the original TV series, Batman. I can remember being so impressed. To me, the producer of Batman was one step removed from God.

Mr. Horowitz and his daughter were very kind to this young Canadian from Toronto. I honestly don't know what happened on any of these nights, or to any of these people, because I was already starting to lose control of my drinking. I just remember thinking, "This is not good. What is wrong with me?"

I would show up at a bar around the corner from our hotel, and the bartender would look at me, then at the clock, which was usually around noon, and say, "Why aren't you on the beach as the others your age?"

I would just stare at him and shrug. I had already crossed over the invisible line of alcoholism: I needed to be there. It was the only way I could settle my nerves; it was the only way I could stay inside my skin.

I was twenty years old. I was already experiencing the jitters and shakes and a very different anxiety. I didn't know what I was afraid of, but this unnamed fear plagued me all the time. That's how it was with me. It was as if I was terrified of failing. I felt we were in over our heads. But I was also determined that I wanted to make it. Success—it was my key to a new life. I'd be 'a somebody' if I could be successful in rock 'n' roll.

I started to miss Beverly Willoughby back in Toronto. Her dad brought her to LA, and we spent a few days showing them around and going to Disneyland. It was wonderful. When they went back to Toronto, I started to get homesick, and I didn't know what to do. By this point, my drinking was progressing. I was into it daily, and my friendly bartender suggested I needed help. But I was not ready to admit it.

Several months later, I returned to Toronto and found out that a young musician was going out with Bev. I was quite upset and jealous, and I headed over to an apartment called the Rose Park. It was near today's St. James Town, at Bloor and Sherbourne.

There, I met this folk singer, Neil Young. I knew his father was a well-respected Canadian journalist, but I didn't know anything about Neil. I'd seen him on one or two occasions at the River Boat Coffee House where he was playing.

I can remember sitting in the living room

with him and Bev, and you could cut the tension in the air with a knife. Finally, I just got up and turned to Bev, and said, "Let's go."

I know Neil liked her. He gave her a sweater filled with colored squares that he made famous, and always wore on stage when he formed Buffalo Springfield shortly after that.

We were all very innocent in those days. I'm sure after Neil became a superstar and I bottomed out on booze at the age of 21, he looked like the one that got away. After that night, however, I never saw him again. But we did hire his brother Bob a few years ago for our Yonge Street series. It all just keeps going around in circles.

7. MARRIED WITH CHILDREN

In early 1968, I married Beverly Willoughby. We moved into her dad's home in Rosedale while a mid-town flat he arranged for us to rent was being renovated. I was drinking every day.

I was working on the floor of the Toronto Stock Exchange. Bert would drive me downtown via Sherbourne and Queen Street. At that corner were the local missions. He would pull his car over, and we would watch the drunks being let out in the morning, many of them sick and hung over, throwing up into garbage cans, or in the park. As we watched them, he would say, "These men weren't born here. Many of them were from good families. They were fathers, brothers, uncles and children of good, kind people. But they have a disease."

I would nod, shake my head in empathy with their plight, and not connect on any level that he was trying to let me know I was headed there if I didn't stop drinking. He was a man with incredible insight.

My brother Jim had originally obtained a position for me as a post boy on the old floor of the Toronto Stock Exchange when I was seventeen years old. Then, after a few years, I started working for a brokerage firm from Montreal. This is where I met Mike O'Shea. He was my immediate superior. He would send the orders down to me on the floor, and I would hand them to the pro trader, Bobby Dunbar. I was in the middle of doing the investment dealers course to become a broker myself.

Every night, all of us would go out to the Savarin Tavern, the old Cork Room or the King Edward's Golliwog Room. I felt like an adult hanging out with all these older stockbrokers and traders. At this point my drinking was completely out of control, even though I was only twenty-one years old. Mike was the only other person close to my age at our firm. We had another friend, Chris, who was also trading on the floor. Together, we would get loaded most nights and end up back at O'Shea's.

My days consisted of working on the floor of the Toronto Stock Exchange and drinking at night. I was driven to earn money in the market, so I could invest in entertainment. That was my goal. But the drinking was getting in the way of my work and my plans. I would head out for a pack of cigarettes and get home two days later.

For Beverly, with a newborn baby, our son Andrew, it was a nightmare. I had no idea why I was doing it, either. I just did these totally unexplainable and irrational things.

Whenever I drank, my personality underwent a tremendous change. I would go from happy-go-lucky to morose. I would become argumentative

After a year of marriage, my wife Bev was on the verge of kicking me out. In March 1969, after alerting my family that I was in serious trouble, my older brother Robert came and had a talk with me. He asked, "Do you think you have a problem with drinking?" "Robert, it's the only thing I have going for me," was my honest response.

In spite of the fact at the age of twenty-one, my hands were starting to shake every morning and I was throwing up every day, I had no idea that I was down for the count. Alcoholism is the only disease in the world that will tell you, "You don't have it." Once you have it, you have it, and all you can do is arrest it. But I didn't know that then.

That's what I honestly believed. I didn't realize that I was in such serious trouble. But I was. I had become my father. My brother suggested I needed help, and I agreed. I was not to stop drinking, however, until March 1970. It was then that I had my last drink of alcohol until this day. Forty-six years.

But it was not the end of my problems. It was only the beginning. In spite of the fact that I'd stopped drinking, in spite of the fact that I'd gone for help, I was so emotionally frail that I couldn't comprehend how damaged I was. The people who helped me stop drinking were not qualified to help me deal with the pain of my childhood, the low self-esteem and the sense of shame that kept me in its grip, or the sense of abandonment I felt. Nothing I did would take away these feelings. I began to read in earnest, looking for the answers in psychology, theology and meditation.

I remember in early 1970 joining a group of friends and going off to a meditation retreat. My new friend Brian and I looked around at the food they'd supplied. It looked liked the feed store at the local co-op. Nuts, grains, rice, tofu.

We looked at the food and at each other,

and slowly made our way to the parking lot, where we jumped into my enormous Buick and raced off to the local Biggy Burger place to get a plain burger and fries. Neither Brian nor I would put anything on the burger, and people would stare at us. He like his burger burnt like shoe leather.

In those days I belonged to the millionaires' club with a group of guys who, like me, were searching for wealth and prestige but were also recovering from drinking.

I called it the millionaires' club because each of us were driving cars we couldn't afford, living in houses we couldn't afford, wondering why our lives were so unmanageable. Back then, I had a phone in the car when it really meant something to have a phone in the car. You had to talk to the radio operator to place your call.

I was never home. I was always working on some deal, which was going to be 'the one' that brought me the fame and fortune I sought. It never came, and we were always in financial difficulty.

I left the brokerage business and tried working in financial planning as part of transforming my life to a young, responsible father/husband. I did quite well and quickly progressed within the sales organization. I was utilizing motivational tapes when I heard of Earl Nightingale. For those who don't know, Earl Nightingale was a wonderful public and motivational speaker. He was brilliant. He had started franchising his work through multi-level marketing.

I was excited by this man's message. It was, for me, the food of life. I talked it over with my wife and the manager of the company I was with, and we decided to start up our own company as a distributor of Nightingale's product.

We formed ASK Corporation, a company selling Earl Nightingale tapes and seminars.

I loved working for myself. I was motivated. I was self-assured for the first time. I was in high gear, and I was going to set the world on fire. But there was no long-term plan in place, and I bounced from crisis to crisis.

In late 1973, after four years of marriage and the birth of my daughter, Colleen, six months before, Bev and I split up. I was devastated. I didn't know what to do. We had been together since our teens, and I was lost. Yet, we also couldn't seem to get along. At this point, it was the darkest period of my life.

For the first time in several years, my friend John Brower showed up on the scene again. One night, he and his wife invited me over to his house. "Want to try some blow?" he asked.

I told him, "I've cleaned up my act. I don't drink or do acid anymore."

He said the words that were to come back to haunt me for the next several years. "Relax. This stuff's not addictive." He then handed me an article from a major US publication that made this claim.

I definitely wasted thirteen years of my life even though I would end up educating myself beyond my own level of comprehension.

8. ON THE ROAD AGAIN

I made the decision in 1974 to head out to the West Coast of Canada to "get my head together." I was already getting in serious financial trouble. I had another relationship blow up because of my substance abuse. I knew I was in trouble again. The only thing I hadn't done was pick up a drink. I made a pledge to myself that I would stick a .45 in my mouth and blow my head off if I ever picked up another drink. That's how terrified I was of alcohol. I also pledged that my children would never see me drunk, as I'd seen my dad. I'm grateful to say they never have.

I headed out of Toronto and hit the Trans-Canada Highway. I was twenty-five years old – going on four years off booze, but totally screwed up. I was lost again. I didn't know where I was heading. I stopped off in Sault Ste. Marie to see my brother Robert, and then I headed west. I had never seen the prairies, and I really enjoyed the sojourn. When I got to Saskatchewan, I decided to do manual labor to try and get in physical shape.

I ended up on a mixed wheat farm outside of Regina. There is nothing like the prairie sky. It is so big and expansive with sunsets that are magical: the sound of crickets, the wind rustling through the wheat fields, and the dead quiet at night.

I worked on the farm for two months. It was a good break. I managed to save a few dollars and to really start getting physically fit. It's amazing what manual labor will do for one's mental health. I began writing daily and keeping journals of my thoughts and feelings. I started doing an inventory of my life. I wanted to work in film. I wanted to get an education. I wanted to write. I still wanted to succeed.

I was in agony over the loss of my children, and I was riddled with guilt about leaving them. I couldn't stop thinking of them, and I would go to bed at night praying for their well-being. I've never experienced heartache the way I did then for Andrew and Colleen, yet I was a complete washout as a father. So I thought.

I was still very angry with God. I still blamed God for the pain in my life growing up. I blamed God for the physical and emotional abuse I'd taken. The idea of trusting God was too much for me, but I yearned for some kind of spiritua awakening. Somewhere in my juvenile mind, had equated God with my father.

The idea of trusting my father was totally incomprehensible to me. That is why I coulc never connect with the concept of God as a loving father. Yet I also wanted to connect to God, if I could.

I soon tired of the farm, and the yearning grew in me to keep moving. I was restless, irritable and discontented. I wanted more. I needed more.

I continued on my journey west. I went to Calgary, which in the early 1970s was a real boomtown. It was still the Wild West – at least for an easterner like myself. I loved Calgary. The Rockies off in the west left an indelible image on my memory. The city was just beginning to develop.

I stayed in Alberta for a few months and decided that I really wanted to keep heading west. I was off to Vancouver. The drive through the Rockies was beyond description. No matter how many times you see the Rocky Mountains on television or in a film, nothing can prepare you for their majesty. When you drive out of Calgary heading toward Banff, the mountains begin to grow and grow, until you find yourself twisting through canyons where the peaks are stratospheric. Occasionally, I would stop just to stare at them—the magnificent ice flows and glaciers reflecting the sun off their pristine white faces, the trees so green and vibrant mixed in with the cascading waterfalls.

I arrived in Vancouver in December of 1974. It was wet and warm for December. I had picked up a hippie and his child hitchhiking outside of Hells Gate, in the Fraser Canyon. Their names were Larry and Zack. Zack would have been about two years old. Larry, like me, was in his mid to late 20s. Here I was a dyed-in-the-wool capitalist—he a true-blue socialist—and we became fast friends. The original odd couple.

I was taken to an apartment in the West End. Vancouver was also in the middle of a development boom in the mid to late 70s. They were building high rises as fast as they could tear down the old homes. In retrospect, it is too bad. They were such beautiful old houses.

At the apartment I met Annie and Betty. They were hippies from Ontario who'd moved west years before. Initially they were skeptical of my values, and me.

I spent countless hours with them arguing

in favor of capitalism over socialism. I pointed ou
I was a Groucho Marxist.

My diet was abysmal at this point. That'
when Betty and Annie decided they were going tc
get me off junk food, even if it killed me. It wa:
the first time in my life I started to get a littl
courageous with food. They lived on stir-fry anc
health food. It was here that I coined the term
Health food kills. I got food poisoning from bad
yeast or something of that nature in one of their
dishes.

During this period I returned to college,
studying journalism, and then transferred tc
Simon Fraser University in Burnaby, British
Columbia, a suburb of Vancouver. The university
was built on the peak of a mountain. You literally
and metaphorically had your head in the clouds.

I began my undergraduate work in
communications. SFU was a tremendous place
to be in the early and mid 1970s. Designed by
Arthur Erickson, it was a forward-looking
institution built entirely of concrete, wood and
glass. It had been built in a hurry. There was an
enormous open courtyard with steps at one end
that led away from the university, and doors at
the opposite end that led into the university. It
had a large area designated for strolling and

sitting, with small shops and services off on each side. There was a campus radio station where I occasionally went on the air.

Dr. Dallas Smythe was a wonderful and wise man who really appreciated my eccentricities and capitalist mentality. He told me I was a capitalist with a conscience. He was a true socialist (dare I say Marxist?) and really did believe wholeheartedly in the importance of dialectic discourse. I was his and Bill Melody's teaching assistant once I was admitted to graduate school, and it was a wonderful period of growth for me.

At SFU, I enjoyed learning. I enjoyed that I was able to be in an environment where it was acceptable to question. I had so many questions. I loved the behavioral sciences. I was intrigued by human behavior, the human condition. It was fascinating to explore the root of our emotional evolution and intellectual advancement. It was also enlightening to question long-held beliefs about our political and economic systems.

Studying the behavioral sciences also allowed me to explore some long-held beliefs. My primary problem was that I kept seeing myself as a rebel. I always needed to be in conflict with others. I was argumentative to the point of boredom. I also hated (and feared) authority and authority figures. They all were highly suspect in my opinion. I viewed them as toxic.

For the next several years, I focused on my studies. During this time I struggled with substance abuse issues from time to time. Unlike Alcohol, I could do some of whatever was going around and then stop. It just didn't affect me the same way alcohol did.

Mike O'Shea moved out to Vancouver at this time. It was good to see an old friend from Toronto. He was now on his way to becoming a partner in a brokerage company.

Web Johnson helped me start up a building maintenance company that gave my friends and me more work and more money, so we wouldn't starve while attending university.

After running the company for six months, I put an advertisement in the paper and sold the business for the next six months of billings. In 1978, this was a lot of money. I moved back into Vancouver from Burnaby, British Columbia, where I'd been living near the university. I was getting back into action.

I bought an old 1958 MGA during this period and began restoring it. Soon I was driving a very distinctive automobile—white with a red interior that everyone would point at, because it was already an antique in 1978. I loved that car. In winter, I had an old English Austin 1100, four-door sedan with front wheel drive. It was great. It burned no gas and was incredibly reliable, especially in Vancouver's climate, which was parallel to the English climate where it had been built. Not too cold, but awfully damp in the winter.

I moved to a very nice apartment on Haro Street, overlooking Stanley Park. The commute out to SFU was now taking me the better part of forty-five minutes, but I enjoyed being back in the downtown core of Vancouver, and not out in the suburbs.

Kits Point (which I am now back living in), in Vancouver was another great place to be in the summer. Looking across English Bay, at the West End was an enclave of hippies and laid-back artists, filmmakers and writers. It was more upscale than the West End. Fourth Avenue had health food stores and great restaurants, as did our little village off Point Grey Road. It also had nice bars where, although I wouldn't drink, I would drop in occasionally.

I was now through most of my MA

coursework, and I continued working as a teaching assistant at SFU. Even though I was only a teaching assistant, it was prestigious to many people outside of academia. It helped my social life, and I was starting to really feel like I was going places. I had small business transactions closing that were providing me with ample financial resources. I got a new Peugeot.

Then my old friend John Brower called me from Newport Beach, California, and said, "Come on down." He'd managed to get a beautiful house on Balboa Island in Newport Beach. I said yes and jumped into my new car and headed to LA. I drove non-stop for eighteen hours, and finally arrived in Orange County. What a place! I loved Newport. I loved the women. I loved the atmosphere, and I loved the ambiance. I met a friend of John's, Jim Goodrich.

He drove a beautiful BMW and was a world-class sailor and racer who traveled around the world in pursuit of adventures. We started to party, and it went on for over two weeks.

Back in Vancouver, I made the decision that I wanted to really get going in business. I was getting tired of university. I wanted to start a film production company. I wanted to write for television. I wanted to be successful.

9. HOLLYWOOD NORTH

In 1979, while I was still in graduate school at Simon Fraser University, I acquired a beautiful house through a friend in West Vancouver. It was on a tiny street called The Dale, overlooking Tidley Cove. It was a lovely house, built on the side of a mountain. I was living with a woman, Betty. She was a very good person who cared about me. She wanted to get married and have kids, and I didn't. She moved out shortly after that.

I wrote a script for a local Canadian television series called The Beach Combers. The producers rejected the script, but somehow one of the editors for the show, the late Frank Irvine, got a hold of my work. He called me and said, "Do you want to meet a young filmmaker who's looking for a partner?" I said, "Yes."

The day I got the call from Phillip Borsos, I arranged to meet him and his accountant, Paul, at my house. Paul was a quiet man, very efficient and had been Phil's accountant for a few years.

He was also a shareholder in Mercury Pictures and Phil's other company, Rocky Mountain Releasing. We sat down and started to talk about what Phillip was looking for and what I wanted to accomplish.

He needed money, and I needed someone with production experience. It seemed like a natural match. I was good at enrolling people in projects, and he was a brilliant young director. I liked him from the moment I met him. He was incredibly bright and had a compelling vision of what he wanted to accomplish. We agreed we would meet again, and I went over to visit Phil alone, without his accountant.

He was living in a third-floor apartment in the West End of Vancouver with his friend, Barry Healey. Barry had just finished directing a short .35mm film, and he was very funny. We would spend countless hours trashing everybody and everything—because while we were geniuses, everyone else was a moron. But it was done with great humor and no real malice.

Healey was writing The Grey Fox at that point. Phil had a small office at 163 West Hastings, right across from Pigeon Park, the name given to it by those on the seedier side of life. It was the beginning of skid row and the lower East Side, filled with drunks, hookers and drug addicts.

It was not a place I would have picked for an office, but eventually, I got to like the location. It became the hub of our little enterprise that was about to spring up from a billboard on the wall of the Keg and Cleaver in Vancouver. As a young boy in Mission BC, Phil had become interested in the tale of Bill Miner.

We agreed on a formula. I was to become the associate producer on The Grey Fox. We agreed on an amount of money that needed to be raised, and I accomplished that. For Phil, according to his friend Barry, it was if he had won the lottery. All of a sudden, he had money. He paid off his debts, and now he was free to develop a feature film. But there was one more problem. He needed a larger sum to pay off a production he was currently producing, and I agreed to raise it for him. For that, I would get forty percent of Mercury Pictures. Phil would have forty-five or so, and Paul would have the rest of the company.

I raised that money. That production was Nails. In 1980, Nails was nominated for an Academy Award, and it felt like we were riding the head of a ballistic missile—however, it was unguided!

Soon Peter O'Brian from Toronto, who was to become the producer of The Grey Fox, joined us as a partner in Mercury Pictures. Peter had completed Outrageous and was looking for his next project.

My brother Jim agreed to help us and introduced me to Bob Crompton and Bruce Cray. I then introduced Phillip to them. We went to Yorkton Securities, where Bruce Stratton agreed to finance half the film.

The big question was whether Peter Brown, the president of Canarim Investments, would agree to fund the other half of the movie. His experience with films had not been good. He was incredibly reluctant but agreed to do help with the financing. In retrospect, we owe our success to those men—my brother Jim, Bob Crompton, Bruce Cray, Bruce Stratton, Peter Brown, and his two partners.

The feature film we started was The Grey Fox. In 1981, I also executive produced Till Death Do Us Part. It came out in 1982 to very favorable reviews.

I can't begin to put into words what it was like getting The Grey Fox made. It would take a book of its own to describe the unbelievably difficult time we endured getting that film finished.

The tax shelter business for Canadian Feature Films was beginning to implode all around us. Pictures were shutting down one after another. Even with the strength of the people we had, our initial financing failed to close. We were in production. We had to go back and re-file our prospectus and start the whole process all over again.

One of the last words Peter Brown said to me was, "If you ever ask me for another dime, I'll punch you in the head."

I can remember thinking, "How much is this going to hurt?" when we had to go back to him again. I walked into his company, Canarim Investments, and he was standing by his office door. He referred to me as Diamond Jim Jr. My brother's nickname is Diamond Jim. He watched me make my way over to Bob Crompton's desk, and then we approached him. I could see the look of "Oh no, here we go again." I think I halfheartedly made a joke to him that I hoped he wouldn't hit me too hard, but we were back and needed his help because our underwriting hadn't closed. Thank God he was a real gentleman.

We persisted, pushing on, day after day. I was originally to have been the associate producer so I could learn how to make a feature Suddenly, I found myself executive producing the film and was responsible for $3.4 million. Given that I was still in graduate school, this seemed like a daunting task. But I was willing to go for it.

A few months before beginning The Grey Fox, I had gone to investigate EST as part of my graduate work in Communication Theory. It was the rage at the time for those looking for instant enlightenment and a way to solve emotional and psychological issues that were preventing you from achieving your goals.

Today it is known as Landmark Forum.

However, at that particular time, it was my belief that EST was a neo-fascist organization or cult that took people in and completely screwed their heads around. With that in mind, my friend and graduate advisor, Bill Richards, and I attended the "training."

I was stunned. It was a very powerful experience. It simply utilized portions of System Theory (Buckminster Fuller, a friend of Gregory Bateson's, was also a great friend of Werner Erhard) and Zen Buddhism combined with elements of psychology. I would discover later on in my research that they had also basically borrowed a lot of technology from L Ron Hubbard's Scientology processes for many of their own.

What they managed to do was illuminate how our minds run us. That is to say, I was not my mind. My mind would say, "You can't do that. You'll never make it. You'll always screw up. No one will like your idea. Who do you think you are?"

It was as if there was a rotisserie in my head that just kept spinning around with all of those negative thoughts on it – only with a strange voice that sounded eerily familiar – like my own. The dialogue was primarily self-defeating thoughts.

All of these thoughts were at the basis of my fears and worries due to the damage done to me in my childhood. Only I was a few years away from discovery the concept of dysfunctional families.

Through the training, I began to realize that my whole life was being run because of messages I had acquired when I was four, five and six years of age. I am not doing a pitch for EST or its successor, Landmark Forum.

But I do give credit to the training and the

Six-Day, which I did subsequently. Those experiences gave me the ability to hang in through The Grey Fox; in spite of the problems we were facing on a daily basis.

Ironically, I just returned and reviewed the Landmark Forum last weekend – after a thirty-seven-year absence. Words cannot express the impact of the Forum. I now realize I probably only "got" about ten percent of what it was they were trying to convey as I had such a closed mind and was in such poor shape mentally, physically and spiritually.

Making The Grey Fox was an emotional roller coaster. For the better part of eighteen months, we would wake up every morning, and it would feel like we would walk out our door, and everyone would take a baseball bat to our psyches and emotions. We were humiliated and laughed at and criticized. The then-head of Canada's Cultural Agency said to me, "At best, The Grey Fox is a mediocre effort."

I wanted to go to the table and punch him in the face. The only problem was he was about six foot three and weighed two hundred plus pounds, and I was five foot ten and weighed about one forty. Instead, I hurled verbal and emotional abuse at him and was ejected from the Canadian

Film Development Corporation's offices and told never to return. Years later I was able to make amends to the gentleman. We both agreed we didn't care too much for one another, but there was no reason we couldn't be civil to each other. Progress.

In the middle of all this, Phillip and I, along with Bruce Cray and Bruce Stratton, headed to Los Angeles for the 1980 Academy Awards. Phil and I were to attend while our financial backers and friends were there for the party if we won. It was an enjoyable experience. The two Bruce's rented a Rolls Royce for us. As we drove up to the Dorothy Chandler Pavilion, the excitement we felt was indescribable. Walking on the red carpet with the cameras flashing and our Canadian Broadcasting Corporation news crew following was surreal.

I felt like somebody for the first time in my life. It was just amazing. When we went inside the theatre and we were shown to our seats, it was a dream-come-true moment.

There were stars everywhere. We followed the ushers, who led us to the back and then up a set of stairs. When we finally arrived at our seats, we were way up in the balcony—so high you could get a nosebleed. I turned to Phil and said, "How long is it going to take you to get down there if you win?"

At that moment, we realized that just being there was our win. It turned out that the winners were all placed on the main floor far below us. Halfway through the ceremonies, Phil and I headed downstairs to the restaurant and ordered chocolate sundaes.

We went back into the awards show and just had a ball. Later that night, we held a party back at the Beverly Wiltshire Hotel. I don't know where they all came from, but we had about fifty people show up. It was a night to remember. I met the Governor of California, Jerry Brown and his then-girlfriend, Linda Ronstadt, who I was madly in love with at the time - only she didn't know that. And I told them that in the elevator. They both laughed and welcomed me to California.

Almost two years later, when The Grey Fox played its first public appearance at the Telluride Film Festival, I knew my life was about to change significantly. Sitting in that darkened theatre, at the end of the film when the audience went completely silent and then erupted in applause, screams and yelling, We knew we had a hit on our hands.

The next year, The Grey Fox won seven out of ten Genie Awards (Canadian Academy Awards) and were nominated for the Golden Globes for Best Foreign Picture and Best Actor with Richard Farnsworth. United Artists Classics had released the film with the help of Fred Roos, who was then heading up Francis Ford Coppola's Zoetrope Studios. We would go on to win the Tourimo Film Festival in Italy, and the hearts and minds of critics throughout the world.

The night The Grey Fox opened in Vancouver was one of the biggest nights in the history of Vancouver's arts scene. Just like Hollywood, they had spotlights outside the theatre, and there was only standing room inside. Everyone was there. For all of us, for Phillip, Peter, Barry, the writer John Hunter, Richard Farnsworth and Jackie Burroughs, it was the ultimate payoff for almost three years of very hard work.

We basked in the accolades of our appreciative audience and friends. The adrenalin rush was overpowering. These feelings were very fleeting. I soon learned that success does have many fathers, and failure is an orphan.

What struck me was how unsatisfactory the whole experience was after opening night.

There was no sense of accomplishment.

I spoke to Phillip about it ten years after the film opened, and he was shocked to learn that it had become one of the most painful periods of my life.

In 1983, Phillip and Peter were starting Father Christmas, which was to become One Magic Christmas for Disney. I was slated to be the executive producer of that film. My drug consumption was out of control. Phillip and Peter sat me down in Toronto and said they wanted me out of Mercury Pictures. In retrospect, I can't blame them. Once again, I had sabotaged myself. The question was why would I do this when I had so much going for me? I was completely baffled.

10. HOLLYWOOD OR BUST

I had already picked up another project, Channel One. Everyone agreed it was a very funny idea for a film fifteen years ahead of its time. It was about how cable and public access would one day overtake traditional broadcasting. I headed to Los Angeles after the first MTV Awards I New York City in 1984. I was seeing a wonderful woman in New York Jo and had met a funny and incredibly talented and intelligent attorney from Boston. He had a Gold Card. I didn't even have a credit card! I asked him what his plans were that week? "Nothing," he said. "Want to come to LA and help put a movie together," I asked? "Sure" was his response. That week turned into a year.

We acquired a very impressive house in West Hollywood, and it was like a traveling circus.

It was at 911 North Alfred, right at Alfred and Willoughby, just east of La Cienega Boulevard. Darla, the girl who had been in the original Little Rascals, lived in it originally, and it had a Bedroom built like Castle that I made into my office.

I had made friends with Alan Sacks through Jo Manuel at the Cannes Film Festival the year of The Grey Fox. Alan had been an executive at ABC and had developed, and executive produced Welcome Back Kotter and Chico and the Man and was now producing feature films. I asked him if he would help us develop Channel One. He agreed. That was the beginning of a friendship that has lasted until today.

Alan was brilliant in his approach to getting the most out of the script. We would work for hours by the pool, where he showed me a system for breaking down scripts that I still use today. We had a great time developing Channel One. With this project, Alan was to introduce me to several key players in Hollywood. I don't remember a time in my life when I laughed so hard or learned so much. In 2003, I would have the privilege of being one of the executive producers of Alan's Disney Channel production of "You Wish."

For the young lawyer from Boston, Bob Rosenblatt, I can safely say it took him a few years to recover from the craziness of that trip to Hollywood. Ironically, Bob is still working with me today, and he recently completed clearing all of our music rights for the Yonge Street Toronto Rock & Roll Stories.

Bob also assisted my partner on Yonge Street, Jan Haust, who recently completed producing Bob Dylan's Basement Tapes out of Toronto. I am very proud of Jan, who just won the Grammy a week ago for that Album. What a great life we've lived.

However, at that time, we were also developing a script by a writer/director, who had Keith Richards from the Rolling Stones agreeing to act as the music producer. Prince, who was red-hot at the moment, had agreed to star, and he had a deal lined up with the Samuel Goldwyn company to distribute the film.

Bob had introduced me to Donald Gadsden, a senior legal counsel at ABC, who, in turn, introduced us to a representative of the Saudi Royal Family. They were referred to as the Saudi Investment Group (SIG). We put together a deal for my new company, Gateway Studios, and the SIG, with me acting as executive producer and Bob and Donald as associate producers. On paper, it was an excellent opportunity.

At the same time, we were introduced to a banker in Los Angeles named Robert Burns. He had agreed and given us written commitment to finance Channel One for $4 million US. We began in earnest to prepare the picture for production.

I brought in my Toronto lawyer, George Flak, and my New York attorney, Alan Vogeler, to Los Angeles along with Bob Rosenblatt to close the financing of Channel One. Stephen Miller, who had introduced us to the man, was present too.

Mr. Burns came into the room, all smiles and chuckles, clapped his hand and said, "Do you know what we are going to do today?"

We all looked at one another somewhat perplexed, and I responded, "Closing our financing."

He shook his head denoting no, and with an almost out of control high-pitched maniacal laugh said, "We're going treasure hunting. I'm financing the hunt for a Galleon off the coast of Florida."

He then looked to all of us for signs of

approval. There was none forthcoming. Once again I had that old sinking feeling. I looked at Alan, Alan looked at George, George looked at Bob, and everyone looked at me, and we all slowly turned and looked at Robert Burns. He just sat there smiling. Waiting for us to acknowledge his plan.

I turned to him. "What about our financing?" "Oh, don't worry about that. How much do you need today?" "Four million dollars," I replied. "No, I mean how much do you need today, right now, to get started?"

We all looked at one another and attempted to get some more clarification. On this day alone we were probably out $20,000 in travel and lawyers fees. George sat down and did a quick calculation about pre-production financing, and we figured we could get going for about $500,000, with the balance to come within a few weeks.

"No problem," said Mr. Burns. "Fine," I said. "Write us a check for $500,000."

He couldn't. He'd need a day or two. A day or two turned into a week, and then two. All the while I had hotel bills at the legendary Chateau Marmont and lawyers' expenses building. Finally, we met Mr. Burns at a landmark Hollywood hotel for lunch.

I sat across from him, and he started up again about this deal and that deal and what he was going to do. I finally blew my stack. I grabbed him by the shirt and physically held him up against a pillar in the hotel dining room.

People around us were somewhat shocked. He broke down and started crying. He admitted he didn't have the funds. He'd been let go by his Bank, and he had a little problem with reality. He just wanted people to like him.

He'd been a friend of Stephen Miller's and had done business with him in the past. We didn't know what to do. Our options were to take his house and leave him on the street.

When we spoke to his wife, she was so distraught that I realized this man was mentally ill. He wasn't capable of discerning right from wrong. And then, it dawned on me just how serious the situation was. We went from optimism to bleak, barren hopelessness in the twinkling of an eye. Thus, trying to close the deal proved impossible, and to this day, the film has never been made in spite of a brilliant screenplay.

The big question was, why did I get into business relationships with people who couldn't be counted on like Mr. Burns? This is a pattern I would repeat several times in my life.

By now we had sunk close to one million dollars of my company and shareholder's money into Channel One. We had to figure out a new game plan—fast! When I told Alan Sacks, he just shrugged his shoulders and said, "Hey, its Hollywood."

Of any person to go through this exercise in futility with me, I am so grateful he was there.

Coincidentally, a director from Portland, Oregon, approached me at this time. He had received my name from someone in Vancouver and showed up at our house/office complex in West Hollywood with Hoyt Axton. Hoyt had just completed Gremlins for Stephen Spielberg; he'd done Heart Like a Wheel and Black Stallion for Carol Ballard.

They were all pictures I liked. Here was Hoyt telling me he'd never done a movie that hadn't either been nominated for an Academy Award or made a hundred million when a hundred million was a hundred million.

When Bob and I read the script for Dixie Lanes, Bob said, "Look, I may only be a lawyer, but this script doesn't seem too good."

His bluntness was one of Bob's most endearing qualities. I thought it was an interesting idea. More importantly, the director had someone with half the financing. I needed to start a film—given that I was now down $908,000 on Channel One, and had no immediate prospects, and the director had a reference from a producer that I admired. When I called Peter, he said, "Yes, the director's a good lad. He has talent. He can do it."

It never dawned on me until later. Why didn't he do it, then?

A script could be fixed. We had Hoyt Axton, the man who'd written God Damn the Pusher Man for Steppenwolf, whose mother had written Heartbreak Hotel for Elvis. I saw an opportunity. It wasn't. Hindsight, however, is always twenty-twenty.

The director brought in a co-producer to protect him from me. Within three weeks of starting, the co-producer strongly suggested we should replace the director.

That was only the beginning of the insanity that was to follow. I wish I'd listened to the co-producer. He went from one hit to another after our film. But here was another pattern: I would be loyal to a fault.

I was to learn from Dixie Lanes—or rather,

I was to grow to accept that I was powerless and that my life was in serious trouble. We ran out of money, and our financing didn't close; we were victims of commercial fraud.

We were being hounded on a daily basis, and we were dealing with private investors again. Every other night I was on a plane…to New York, to Toronto, to San Francisco…and by the time we completed shooting the last week of October 1986, I was running on empty. I had left a few weeks before we wrapped, leaving the crew, the co-producer and the director to shut down the production while I scrambled around New York trying to put together the last of the financing. I had no luck for six months, and the heat was building for me to find a solution. At this point, "bleak, barren hopelessness" was starting to look good to me as I descended into fear, terror, sheer terror, and then complete hopelessness.

Once again, George Flak came through and was able to arrange close to three-quarters of a million dollars in post-production financing.

It was based on the successes I'd had with Grey Fox and Till Death Do Us Part. We were put through the meat grinder in Seattle trying to satisfy all the creditors. Time and time again, the whole project came within seconds of collapsing.

There was so much distrust swirling around the production that it started to look like we'd never get the film finished. Through the help of another law firm in Seattle, which Alan Vogeler arranged, George Flak and the Seattle lawyer were able to negotiate a deal with our creditors.

The Attorney General and our co-producer agreed to have the negative move to Canada to complete postproduction. If it were to sit in Seattle, it was unlikely anything would have ever happened with it, because the negative was a lightning rod for litigation.

I returned to Toronto to finish the film. In Toronto, I met the woman I would end up marrying. It turned out that Deb thought I was a complete flake. I pursued her for months on end while she rejected every advance I made. That's all I'd ever heard in life, and I never actually took NO to mean NO from anyone. It just meant no, not now to me. Finally, she acquiesced and went out with me. Our first date was one of my screenings of Dixie Lanes. She hated it. But she didn't know how to tell me. She asked a friend of both of us what she should do. Sue said, "Lie if you like him."

I had fallen head over heels in love with her. Besides my children, she is the best thing that has ever happened to me, and I am so grateful I had her in my life for twenty years. We moved in together and set up house.

My second trip after visiting my hometown with Deb was to the LA Film Market in the spring of 1988. Here, I finally recognized that the only real thing about Dixie Lanes was that it was in focus and that the sprocket holes were in the right place.

With this revelation, I curled up in the fetal position in The Good Night Inn on the 101 North of LA and wished I could disappear. There was no more Chateau Marmont for me.

At the screening were several hundred of my creditors, cast and crew, as well as buyers. As the movie ended, there was a riotous reaction from the audience, who were just grateful I'd finished the film and now saw a possibility of getting their money back.

Several Video buyers were apparently mystified. While the movie didn't appear to be very good to them, we would be paid a significant amount of money for ancillary rights, such as video, because of the audience's reaction. Unfortunately, the video company never recovered their initial investment and soon went out of business.

Deb cared for and nurtured me through that bout of ontological implosion. One minute I was strolling down the street, brimming with self-confidence, the next filled with fear. I had the emotional stability of nitroglycerine at that point in my life.

Dixie Lanes was my Waterloo. At the premiere in Milan, Rona Wallace, an old friend of Bob Rosenblatt's and who had been the vice president of MGM Video when we rented her home in Beverly Hills, came to the screening.

She fell asleep on my shoulder twenty minutes into the film. Even I knew this was not a good sign. I remember heading back to my hotel in Milan, looking out the window and thinking, "I should jump." The trouble is, with my luck at that point, I would have ended up paralyzed and helpless, and not dead. We were heading out the next day for Venice, and the thought crossed my mind, "Death in Venice: Part Two."

When I returned to Toronto from Europe, it was the start of the hardest period I had faced until then. I didn't get a night's sleep for over a year. Every day, people called me and threatened to sue me. Eventually, I became immune to threats. I remember a creditor from Los Angeles calling and starting to scream, and I quietly said,

"You have two choices: you can stop screaming and talk calmly, and I will listen, or I will hang up."

He screamed back, "Well, you listen to me, you scum bag, I'm going to sue you. How do you like that?" I quietly said, "Take a number. I believe you are 604. Good luck."

I calmly hung up the phone, and a few hours later he called back. "You weren't kidding, were you?" I was not. It would take me over five years but eventually, every lawsuit was dropped, and I have gone on to repay or find acceptable terms on almost 90% of the money that was owed. I am still sending cheques out today – thirty years later. But I have my integrity intact.

In closing this chapter, here is what I know today. I don't believe any of us choose our parents, but we can choose how we react to them. None of us is responsible for how our parents acted or reacted to us growing up.

Most of us are making decisions about our lives from the point of view of a three to twelve year-old—except for those fortunate few that seem to be totally well adjusted and mature. And they are out there. You may be one of them. Perhaps what I am about to embark on will help you understand the friend or family member who doesn't think like you.

That is my hope. The next section of this book will outline to you exactly how I came to change my beliefs, my attitudes, and my way o life.

I have a life today that is good. Is it perfect? No. But it's a lot better than it ever was. No longer am I plagued by fear all the time. I don't lie awake at night worrying about my future the way I once did. I don't beat myself up regularly for making mistakes. Today, you can count on me to do what I say I will do. Am I perfect? No, but there has been marked and significant improvement.

Today, I believe I am worthy. I do deserve to have a happy and peace-filled life. I think it's all right to have sufficient material and financial resources to live comfortably. I believe there are enough resources in the world for everyone. I do believe in sustainable growth–emotionally, intellectually and financially. I believe that we can turn our lives around and have supportive, loving and happy relationships. I believe we can save our planet. We can have peace on earth.

How did I get here, you ask? By taking the first step.

11. I SURRENDER –STEP ONE

I surrender. I admit that, of myself, I am powerless to solve my problems, powerless to improve my life. I need help.

There are many ways to enlightenment. One can walk, run, drive or fly. No matter which mode of transportation you choose, they will all eventually get you to the same place. That's why today, I've stopped judging people and organizations that teach or guide one to a better way of life. I don't believe any religion, philosophy, or movement of any kind has the market cornered on gaining insight into human behavior. I think there is one God and many paths to him, or her, or it.

One spiritual plan I did run across—which is just about the simplest but most efficient path—was that of the late Jack Boland and his eight steps to Master Mind Consciousness. I never personally met the man, but I did get to know him through his writings, his audiotapes and through my interaction with some friends when we decided to follow his Master Mind

Principles, and form a Master Mind Group.

And I am still using the principles almost twenty years after I found them. Jack was also a fellow traveler. He knew and understood defeat and surrender. He knew pain intimately. The pain of loss, rejection and failure. He turned his life around and became a Unity minister. I love the work of another one of Unity's ministers Catherine Ponder. I have read and will continue to read on a daily basis her book, Open Your Mind to Prosperity, for nearly thirty years.

Many years ago I sent Catherine Ponder a note, and she was kind enough to respond. My question had to do with free will and to surrender my beliefs about free will, God, and prosperity. This belief is an area that I am often torn by guilt. It's not okay for me to have wealth. It's not okay to want to have a sailboat, a nice car, and a beautiful home for my family when so many people are starving or doing without the necessities of life. I couldn't bring myself to reconcile how it is okay for us in the west to be consuming so many of the world's natural resources while thousands of children die every minute of every day in Africa and South Asia because of hunger.

As I mentioned earlier, I had developed a

substance abuse issue after stopping drinking. It was on April 18, 1987, that I hit bottom.

On Holy Thursday of 1987—the day before Good Friday, according to the Catholic tradition in which I was raised— I stood in Washington Square Park in New York City. In those days, it was a drug supermarket. You could get anything you wanted, and it was all out in the open. I bought some pot.

I was grappling with the thought of getting high again. However, I also wanted to change the direction of my life for good. I was utterly desperate because I wasn't able to raise the money yet to finish Dixie Lanes.

I turned and walked out of the park over to Sixth Avenue. I stood on the corner of Sixth and Waverly, looking at the old apartment of my former girlfriend, Jo. I was filled with regret and sorrow.

To this day, I still do not know what happened, but here's how it unfolded. I stood just off Washington Square Park looking uptown at Sixth Avenue. A voice inside of me that was as clear as a bell said, "You'll die if you start on drugs again."

Without knowing why I threw what I had on

me in a garbage can and started walking uptown
I crossed over to Fifth Avenue. My mind was
racing. I couldn't think straight. I just knew
needed help

What I find mystical, and somewha
peculiar, is at that moment in Toronto, a very old
friend of mine, Jack Humphrey, lay in his house
in Rosedale, dying.

Jack and I had stopped drinking at the
same time seventeen years before.

We had remained good friends, and it was
Jack who told me I could be the funniest writer in
Canada. He was producing such Canadian series
as King of Kensington, Hanging In and Flappers
and had just started executive producing Silver
Spoons for NBC when he was diagnosed with lung
cancer.

When I found out he'd died a
approximately the same time I threw the po
away; it sent a chill down my spine.

I thought I would talk to my lawyer, Alan
Vogeler. It was a long walk uptown to Rockefeller
Plaza. I kept reflecting on the mess I'd made of my
life, the relations I'd harmed, my children and my
mother. I looked up, and I was standing outside
St. Patrick's Cathedral. I walked inside, found a

pew and sat down. I dropped to my knees, tears streamed down my face, and I said, "If there is a God, please help me."

I left St. Patrick's and walked across Fifth Avenue to Rockefeller Centre and up to Alan's office. I went in and told him I was in serious trouble. He thanked me for my candor and asked me what I was going to do. I told him I was going to try and get clean.

I called a new friend of mine, Linda, and headed up to her apartment. We'd met months before on a wet Friday night in Manhattan when we both tried to hail the same cab. In New York,

little old ladies have been known to assault very large men to hold onto 'their' cab. She was a real diplomat and said, "Why don't we share this taxi?" After that, we had become friends and even enjoyed a brief romantic relationship, but I was too fragile when I met her and not available. At least, I had been honest with her, and as a result, we had remained friends.

I called her, and she told me to come over. She was going out of town for the weekend but told me to make myself at home. I explained that I couldn't go back to my apartment.

It was a dangerous place for me because my

dealer would inevitably show up and call me with the words, "I'm downstairs."

I was always powerless to say no to him and it would send me off again on another binge. I never returned to that apartment. I just left all the furniture, my clothes, carpets, stereos and personal belongings; because I knew I would fail if I went back. I had to be willing to go to any lengths to straighten my life out.

On Friday morning, Linda got up, checked on me and made me coffee and toast. Everyone who knows me will laugh at this recognition.

I lived on toast and cereal. Long before Seinfeld made an issue of it, I survived on that combination. I was unbelievably shaky. I felt sick to my stomach.

My head hurt, my hair hurt. I just put one foot in front of the other. I had a yearning to go to Good Friday Mass. Linda is Jewish but agreed to go with me to keep me company before she left town.

It was very cold that April 18th. There was a brisk wind blowing along West End Avenue that chilled me to the bone. I had never bothered to get myself a proper New York or East Coast winter coat. I had a Barney's trench coat, which I wore all winter. I froze—but I looked good. It was always important to me to look good. I inherited that trait from my father, too.

We went to a small Catholic church on the Upper West Side. As I sat contemplating my life, I was overcome with a sense that I had surrendered. There was no more fight left in me. My need for terminal uniqueness was lifted right out of me that morning. At that moment, I yearned for normalcy. I just wanted to stop hating myself, and to forgive myself for having destroyed so many wonderful opportunities.

I surrendered my ego to the idea of God because I couldn't figure out who or what God was. I have come to accept that when my ego is in full force,

It is hard for me to connect on any spiritual level. EGO=Edge Good Out - Edge God Out! My ego was responsible for my inability to accept my powerlessness over drugs

. My ego kept me locked into self-destructive, self-sabotaging behavior. It had been useful as a child when I needed it to survive: to reinforce that I was okay and deserved to live. But now it had turned on me. It was dangerous to my survival. Often people confuse humility with humiliation. They are not the same. Often

humiliation can lead to humility, but not always
I had to let go of a lot of beliefs in that small
church. I needed God more than God needed me
I needed help in the worst way.

We returned to Linda's apartment, and she
prepared to leave town for Easter weekend. She
had Shirley MacLaine's videotape of Out On a
Limb, which I'd never seen. I sat and watched it
a state of bewilderment. I didn't necessarily
subscribe to any of Ms. MacLaine's beliefs at that
time, but I must confess, right then, I was grateful
to see that show. I put it back in the machine and
played it over several times that weekend. What
was important to me was the message: when I try
and run my life, I end up in serious trouble and
my life was a train wreck.

I have to surrender and believe in
something outside (or inside) of me. It is
imperative if we are to find the happiness that we
come to see that there is a Power greater than we
are. At this stage of my life, I was agnostic.

I wanted to believe, but all my education
all my experiences in life told me it was wishful
thinking. It would be nice if there were a God and
an afterlife, but the fact was, I believed that all
that happened after we died was that a part of us
survived in our children. That's what I believed

that day. I knew I had to believe in something. As I stated earlier, God could be as simple as Good Orderly Direction.

Two years later I was sitting and talking to my friend, Tim McCauley, and his friend, John Heard, who starred in Out on a Limb. I told him how much the show had helped me. John laughed and shared how he was in a dark place himself when he'd made it. He was going through his own 'dark night of the soul' in the area of relationships. It hadn't registered at that level with him, but it's interesting to see how he did work that he never knew would end up possibly helping to save another human being's life.

Later that year, George Flak invited me to a luncheon at the Bel Air Hotel in Los Angeles for Canada's former Prime Minister, Pierre Trudeau. I was able to share with his escort, Shirley MacLaine, how much I'd been helped by the show.

I always thought that those two events were tied into the miracle of my recovery.

But back in New York that Easter weekend, I was in desperate shape. I knew I wanted to get better. I knew I had to go back out to California, where I was sharing a house in Malibu with my old friend John Brower. I was terrified that he and

I would start partying, and that would be the end of my sobriety.

I crawled onto the plane a week later and flew back to LA. It was early May. I had just met with George Flak and his friend, Nick Stiliadis, and they agreed to fund the completion of Dixie Lanes. We would release it as an SC Entertainment Picture. In that regard, I felt like a thousand-pound weight had been lifted off my shoulders. At least now I could get the film finished, and hopefully, pay off all of my creditors and get my life to a place I'd never been: sane and clean.

When I arrived at the airport, John picked me up. He and I had shared apartments and houses in LA for years. I would pay part of the rent so I would have a place to stay when I arrived in town. First was the Hollywood Hawaiian, all those years ago with Bob McBride. Then there had been an apartment in West Hollywood, and then a gorgeous house in Beverly Hills, on North Beverly Glenn Drive.

Now we had a great beach house on Old Malibu Road. When I told him that I had to stop using, he just looked at me and said, "I was worried about having to talk to you."

He had come to the same realization while

I had been in New York.

I was torn about going back to Toronto. While my family and my kids from my first marriage were there, the city had a lot of bad memories for me. But if I wanted to finish Dixie Lanes, I had to return. I created a plan of action. I would call some old friends that I knew I could trust. I would tell them the truth about what kind of shape I was in, and I would surrender to their direction. I would trust these people because I couldn't trust myself, or God, quite yet. I wanted to, but I just couldn't. It was in April 1987 when a young lady I was friend's with in Malibu gave me a copy of Catherine Ponder's book, Open Your Mind to Prosperity.

At this point, I still believed that money would solve my problems. I kept thinking it was the millions I owed that was the deep, underlying issue. It was not. However, the book contained a series of prayers that gave me comfort. They enabled me to come to believe that I was worthy and that I could have what I needed, and I began to see that prosperity meant a lot more than just money.

This thought was an entirely new concept for me. I never thought of spiritual prosperity where I had enough...enough money to live on for that day, enough food to eat for that day, enough love from my wife and children to do me that day

We had a home. I had friends who truly loved me when I couldn't love myself. I had friends who were willing to support me, as long as I was going to put the effort into changing my way of life and my way of thinking.

Change is not easy. It can be very painful It is frightening. If you don't feel it- you can't hear it. Do not be afraid to face your demons and if you can, just experience the feelings you without self-judgment. It is the only way I know of to heal We have to go through the pain to leave it behind There is no easy way out. But we also need support, which is why a Master Mind Group or self-help or support group that deals with families of alcoholics can be so helpful.

We need to acknowledge ourselves for taking the risk to change. For many of us, our behavior is something we learned as children that supported us when we were young. It is how many of us survived. To give up that behavior and head into the untried territory is bedlam.

I felt nervous and excited about returning to Toronto. It had been years since I'd left, and I had no idea what to expect. John Brower had arranged with a friend of his for me to sublease her apartment at Bay and Bloor. It was a very central location, and it turned out that one of my oldest friends lived in the same building. His friends referred to him to as the 'spiritual giant'.

He was someone I could trust and count on for guidance. He and my old friend Brian helped me get back on my feet. It was with this friend who, along with Brian, I'd gone on the meditation retreat seventeen years before.

He had also been doing some work on himself, and had come across a program about healing the pain of our childhoods by using a writing workbook. He too had an alcoholic father who was abusive. Like me, he also had to deal with an incredible sense of shame. I said to him about self-esteem, low self-esteem would have been a significant uptick for me. I had no self-esteem.

We attended an information meeting and decided to take the workshop. That decision was one of the turning points in my life. I had to start looking at my powerlessness in a number of areas besides substances. I had to see how I was powerless over relationships, my need to control, my need to be overly critical and judgmental. I was powerless over perfectionism. I have come to realize today that perfectionism is perhaps the most destructive form of self-abuse.

My mind said, no one would be able to do it as well as me, so, therefore, I had to do it all. Of course, I would soon become angry and resentful at anyone I was in a relationship with, or working with, because I had to do it all.

The best example of what I am talking about is the insanity of getting on an airplane, of which I have a fundamental knowledge of how they fly, yet having the need to go up and make sure that the pilot's doing it right. How in the hell would I know what right is, if I've never been trained? But I sure wanted to go up there and check it out. My friends and I attended these writing workshops for twenty-six weeks. It was extremely powerful and extremely painful at times, and finally, it was liberating.

So, surrender took on many meanings to me. First, it was that I was powerless over alcohol and drugs; next, I was powerless over my finances and my career.

I was powerless over unhealthy relationships—I would continue to go to people who were incapable of giving me what I needed, especially in business.

I was powerless over what my children from

my first marriage thought of me, or what my ex-wife thought of me. I was powerless over the thoughts that came into my mind about what I had done in my life. But I was not powerless over what I did with those thoughts if I got help.

I had to temporarily surrender my business and my goals so I could re-contextualize my life. I needed a new set of values because apparently my old ones weren't working. The therapist I was seeing, Dr. Rose, pointed out to me that I needed a complete overhaul in the way I viewed life and success.

Clearing up the wreckage of our pasts is not an easy task. It is painful, and it is slow. But it must be done if we are to receive any peace of mind. It is well worth the price of admission to get back on a healthy footing with those we love.

When I returned to Dr. Rose, he pointed out I also had to change my priorities. As an example, when I was in serious financial difficulty and several months behind on our rent, I was offered a position with the Canadian Broadcasting Corporation's Newsworld.

This network was a new Canadian news service like CNN, only with a Canadian perspective. I love news. It's why I had studied Journalism first in college. When I went to him full of excitement, he simply looked at me and said, "Find a new therapist if you take that job."

I was devastated. I couldn't understand why he was saying this to me when I needed money so desperately. I'd gone to my friend George Flak to get the job in the first place "Why?" I demanded out loud.

"Because you need to work on yourself." He pointed out that, in his opinion, I would probably die if I went right back into a pressure-cooker situation. If I wanted to get better, I had to follow his lead and begin examining my life in its minutiae. I had to work on my life before I worked for a living.

"Here we go again," was my initial reaction. I just thought it was all BS. My mind went insane with anger. Nobody understands me." I started to get unhinged. How wrong I was—again. I don't know why, but I listened to the good doctor, and today see the wisdom in his advice.

Finally, in late 1987, I got to a place where I understood I was powerless, and I was beaten. I could not find a way to solve my problems on my own. It was pointed out to me that my best thinking—the actual most brilliant thoughts I had ever had—finally put me in this place. I had to surrender my old way of thinking completely.

Here is the greatest single realization I've had: Once I accept that I am powerless, I begin to receive the power – the power to recovery from a seemingly hopeless state of mind and body. It is the ultimate paradox, we surrender to win.

12. I BELIEVE – STEP TWO

I believe. I come to believe that a power greater than myself, the Master Mind, can change my life.

Let me start off by saying that I didn't have a very serious problem with organized religion and God in my adolescence and early adult years. I've just never been able to connect with the concept of a loving higher power as a father figure. I wish I could today. To me, my father meant potential death. Subsequently, I couldn't hear the message. I couldn't respect authority figures, and if there was one thing the Catholic Church I was raised in was, it was authoritarian.

I had grave doubts about the existence of God. One of the great things about education is that it enables one to learn how to think critically and not accept precepts just on faith. To enter into dialectic discourse—to question, to ponder and wonder where I fit in the grand scheme of things, is one of the great intellectual rewards of a higher education. It's also one of its biggest pitfalls.

The further I went with my education, the less I believed in anything anymore. I had to be able to prove it empirically. At one time, I'd been involved in the Charismatic Renewal in the Catholic Church.

I liked those people. I believe they were genuine and open.

There are men like Zander Dunn, a Presbyterian minister on Amherst Island where I used to live, who carries God's message of love and forgiveness. The same for the local Catholic priest, Father Grainger, who was there at the time. He was a very kind and insightful Catholic Priest. The same is true for Andrew Chisholm at the Anglican Church. I recently attended a Jewish funeral, and that service struck me as being remarkably compassionate.

Be aware of black or white thinking: all or nothing. It is unhealthy psychologically. At its root are perfectionism and pride. No one can live up to the person who has perfectionist ideals or standards. It is a form of codependency that has people operate out of shame and blame. The good news to me today is that I have come to believe that a power greater than myself—The Master Mind—can change our lives. When we choose to sit with one other person, the Bible says, "When two or more are gathered, then I am there too."

I paraphrase for the benefit of any pedantic people who insist on exact quotes. I don't think it matters to God what you call him. As long as you know it is God you are speaking to - I can't imagine He or She cares.

When I was in Jerusalem, I was standing in the square that looks over the Dome of the Rock, the Wailing Wall and the Church of the Holy Sepulcher, I had a revelation. My personal epiphany was that the founding of three of the world's most predominate religions was within a five-iron of each other. In case, you're not a golfer that is a very short distance.

In communication theory, there is the concept of Punctuation of Sequence of Events. If you take three people, all standing on different corners, and ask them to describe the same event that just transpired—whether it is a car accident or debate—you will be given three distinct and unrelated answers. If you didn't know they'd been standing in the same corner or present at the same accident, you would never have guessed it. So, here we had a variety of very spiritual individuals, two of them ironically are first cousins (The Jews and Palestinians), who all heard the same message and interpreted it differently.

We all agree there is one God who is great, but we all choose to call Him by our ethnocentric names. In fact, for us Westerners, Jesus' name was changed from Yeshua, probably between 300 to 500 CE.

In my work as a writer, producer, and director I have investigated various subjects: Is there life after death? Are there angels? Does some part of our consciousness survive after death?

What about hell? Does it exist? What about reincarnation? Do we come back?

Having spent years in the field talking to people who underwent Near Death Experiences, who had seen manifestations of deceased loved ones as well as scientists, doctors, and skeptics—that the evidence was overwhelmingly for the fact that something extraordinary does happen at the time of death. There is no doubt in the minds of those people who have had one of these experiences that it was real.

There are mysteries out there that have no natural explanation. From a purely medical point of view, many of the people we met and interviewed and who had these remarkable experiences should not have lived or survived the traumas they did. Time and time again, I met the physicians who confirmed that fact. Here they were. These were sane, conservative, rational people in every area of their lives—except for these occurrences, which defied all known scientific explanation. And they all came from a variety of religions and theological backgrounds but not all believed in God.

The researchers and quantum physicists who are working on these questions are just as puzzled as anyone because they know that something quite remarkable is happening. The challenge that faces the scientists in this field is they can't replicate these studies in the traditional, empirical paradigm they usually operate within.

Therein lies the mystery of it all, and that's where faith is needed.

When I didn't believe in God, I lived in constant fear. In spite of tremendous success in my chosen profession, I never had more than a fleeting experience of happiness. I was driven to want more. I had no peace of mind, and I was riddled with jealousy and resentment. Why couldn't we get what we wanted? I always had to deal with people that had never done what we had done creatively but had the power to approve what we were about to try and do.

I love Hollywood or the image of Hollywood. It gave me a chance to see that one could acquire tremendous success, and it still didn't guarantee happiness. What is ironic to me is that I was never very happy with the whole process of doing theatrical feature films. There were moments of elation, but no sense of accomplishment. I wish I could have changed the way I felt. But, it was not to be.

When I finally hit bottom after the debacle of Dixie Lanes and realized we were in big trouble, I didn't know what to do. When I was back in New York City, as I wrote earlier, I felt overwrought. I began to question if I could ever change. Would my life ever stop being in chaos and shambles?

I was supposed to be enjoying the benefits of our films and the critical success of our previous productions. Instead,

I was frantically, desperately trying to get another movie made. I was like a junkie who needed another filmic fix. I knew if I could get one more, my life would be different. Just like all the other times I believed: once I get a new girlfriend, the right car, the right address, the right deal, the right haircut, the right clothes, the right friends, the right city, the degree or degrees, the right amount of money—well, then, you'll see everything will be just great, fabulous. But it never comes.

There's never enough when all we seek is material wealth, possessions or the acknowledgment and praise of the world. There is no lasting benefit to it. Even though these statements have been pointed out in every inspirational book written in the last several thousand years, I feel as if I just found out, and wow! What a great realization it is to come to in my right mind!

But what does last is a belief in a power greater than we are, and a desire to be of service. It gives one purpose. It allows us to experience the pain of change sufficiently, so we can break free of the bondage of self. We can finally let go of the need to prove ourselves to others. We're okay just the way we are.

We don't have to become a hotshot producer, writer, doctor, lawyer, poet, candlestick maker, public servant. Becoming the president of a major corporation,

famous politician, or any other 'thing or occupation' that we think is not going to change our lives or us if we don't have a rock solid and healthy foundation under us.

When we change at our core and become loving, patient and generous human beings, capable of forgiving the worst enemy or the best friend, when we can let go of anger and resentment, incredible events come to pass. All we have to do is keep showing up and asking for help. Then if we still want it, chances are we can get back into the game of life. We can undertake projects to be of service—to entertain, to educate or enlighten—then we're on the right path and can expect the best results. We can have all the success we want, and enjoy it.

Life ebbs and flows, and I've noticed as the Byrds' song once said back in the 60s, there is time for planting and a time for harvesting, a time for living and a time for dying.

We don't necessarily always have to die physically. We can suffer emotional death through depression, rejection or the loss of a loved one. But rebirth—the concept of resurrection—is a beautiful notion to live our lives by. We do rise again. We do come back if we just don't quit one day too soon.

No matter how bad life is today, if we put the effort in to change, I can promise you that it will be that good tomorrow

. In other words, the degree that you are hurting today will be the degree of happiness that you will gain by surrendering and believing in a Power greater than you.

Do we ever stop making mistakes or being weak-willed? Not that I can see. The only things I've done perfectly for the past 30 years is not use any mind-altering substance. But I've just about done everything else wrong that a human being can. Each mistake I've made has contributed to my growth. Embrace change. Make mistakes. They all lead to the right answer eventually.

Worrying about making mistakes keeps us locked into unhealthy perfectionist thinking, and expectations about others and ourselves.

Coming to believe in a Power greater than you is the best formula I know of to change our lives. If you could have your concept of God, what or who would it be?

I'm not deprecating material achievement. Given the choice, I'd rather live any day in comfort, surrounded by beauty and nice possessions. I enjoy a beautiful home, which I have today. I enjoy driving nice cars.

One of the toughest areas in our lives that we have to work hardest on is that we are worthy human beings. We deserve a nice home, good transportation. We deserve a good income. We deserve a happy and peaceful family life. We deserve to be debt free.

These are affirmations I must continue to feed into my mind, like you would a new software program into a computer, to counteract all of the negative messages I received in my childhood. In my case, my brain is like a corrupted hard drive, so I must reboot it with fresh software every morning as it's all corrupted again by the end of the day. The fresh software is the eight steps.

Here's the crux of the problem for me. When we keep chasing money or a career at the cost of our personal life and our relations, it is counter-productive. When we are never home because we are a workaholic, it is hard on our children and our relationships. Furthermore, when our only focus is on obtaining material possessions to make ourselves feel better, or to be acceptable to society or our peers, the experience is empty, hollow and leads to just wanting more.

We can never fill the emotional hole we feel inside ourselves with material possessions. No matter how much we buy, it is never going to be enough. Those beliefs are the lies my mind tells me. I don't have the right possessions, but if I go to the right store, then, this time, you will be happy. I won't, you won't, and it will never happen.

Balance is the key. When we believe in a Power greater than ourselves, when we believe that this Power can change the way we think, feel and act, we are finally on the road to liberation.

We will begin to know joy and happiness that we've never experienced. We will be able to forgive ourselves for being human and making mistakes. We will not be plagued by perfectionism. We will become more patient and loving, or, at least, more so than we ever were. If you want to find out how you're doing in life, ask your immediate family or your romantic partner. Do they share the same vision of your life as you do? Good question. Be grateful for what you already have. Give thanks frequently for the things that matter in your life, like your health and the health of your family. Write a list on the front of a notebook or your day timer, and look at it every day.

It is good to ask God to guide us in all our affairs. If we come to believe, then we can turn over our relationship with the man or woman we want in our life. Mind you; there is no one at the moment, but I believe I will be guided to the right woman when the time is right. I hope!

When we ask a Higher Power to guide us, we are given peace when we would regularly blow up and overreact, most of time. If we do blow up, which I do occasionally now, I can admit I was wrong and apologize to my sweetheart, co-workers or kids. We can be more patient with our children and our friends.

When we believe in God, we can let go of results in life: writing exams, getting a job, acquiring a raise or promotion, or in my case,

writing this book or waiting for networks or studios to get back to me on projects.

We can ask to be guided in our choice of a career. We can ask for help in our family relations. Feuds of long standing can melt away miraculously and mysteriously when we release the results. We will find that we are filled with a new sense of optimism about the future, regardless of what the previous circumstances were.

You may have deep-seated emotional and mental problems. They can be helped too. All it takes is a willingness to believe.

The question I have is, what do you have to

lose by trying it for ninety days? Find a group o
like-minded people. They are everywhere
Churches, social gatherings, service clubs like
Rotary or the Lions Club or any of the myriad o
other philanthropic organizations that are always
seeking active and caring people. They are people
just like you and me looking for answers. The
common bond that holds many of us together is
that we want to be of service.

Many of these organizations also believe in
God, as you understand him or her to be. As a
result of our beliefs, our lives have been changed
at every level: spiritually, emotionally, physically
and financially.

13. I AM READY TO BE CHANGED – STEP THREE

I realize that erroneous self-defeating thinking is the cause of my problems, unhappiness, fears and failures.

I have been plagued my whole life with self-doubt, low self-esteem, and a fear of failure. People who don't know me are often shocked when I say these things. "How can that be when you've done so well?" is the most common question I'm asked.

These feelings and emotions have immobilized me at times, and at others, caused me to overreact in very unhealthy ways. When filled with fear, we become too aggressive. In compensating for these feelings, we can become arrogant, while filled with insecurity. Many people in Hollywood operate out of this psychological model. I refer to it as "egocentric megalomaniacs with low self-esteem."

It is best summed up in an old Zen saying "An empty vessel makes the loudest noise." It i imperative to realize that self-defeating thinkin; is the cause of most problems, unhappiness fears and failures in life.

What are the traits that keep us locked int this behavior? First: thinking of ourselves as a victim. I was victimized as a child, and unconsciously I've carried that into my adult life It is neither healthy nor constructive, and it car be changed. We have often blamed others for the way we feel. Many of us have never stood up fo ourselves when we have been wronged. We've been afraid to tell people what we really think fo fear of rejection. I didn't want anyone else rejecting me...after my father had.

But giving away one's power—that is, no taking care of ourselves appropriately—leads to depression, anger and resentment. If we don' know how to take care of ourselves, how can we ever hope to properly enter into an equa partnership with another human being, whethe it's our wife, life partner, a business partner or a true friend? If we don't change, we will lack integrity and courage, because we're always a the whim of what others think of us. We're afraid to take a stand, or we only take stands in order to dominate and be popular. Once again, extremes seem to play an integral part in this way of being.

Being a victim also creates the potential for rage—misappropriate rage at the wrong people, at the wrong time, in the wrong places. How do we cope with these feelings? We begin to utilize inappropriate activities to change the way we feel. We seek highs in work, alcohol, drugs, food, or sex, to name just a few.

We become chronic overachievers, who are constantly left with depression, because once the high of the accomplishment is gone, we are left with these uneasy feelings of inadequacy. This paradigm leads to 'all or nothing' thinking.

We often seek out individuals or situations that are not healthy for us, or unavailable to us. When we achieve what we want from them, then we withdraw, hurting them and others. When we are attracted to relationships or seek out persons who are not available to us, it is a form of juvenile selfishness and self-centeredness.

When we don't get what we want, we withdraw and become reclusive. We isolate, feeling sorry for ourselves. We plot revenge, or we gossip with the intention of destroying reputations and careers by spreading untruths.

This can only lead to depression and will always come back on you or me—in exactly the same form as we put it out. It may take years, but I guarantee, it will happen. What is at the root of this dilemma? Number one is pride, followed closely by fear, resentment and envy.

What happens is, we become afraid of being less than perfect. We won't allow ourselves to go to social or work events and enjoy the company of our wife or romantic partner, for fear of not being liked by her friends or fear that we may be judged by others because we don't have the right job, or we don't wear the right clothes.

We may not have traveled in the right social circles growing up. Or, like me, you may have been someone that grew up in a good neighborhood, but you were the only child whose parents had separated, or your mother had to work like mine did, while all the other kids parents had professional or executive occupations. These kinds of feelings, these insecurities from our childhoods, stay with us and haunt us in our mature years.

You may feel insecure about your economic future because your colleagues at work may judge you harshly. As a result of your inability to socialize, your job may be at risk—especially if you have an occupation that demands we interact socially. In truth, what is being threatened is our self-esteem and our financial future. That really crippled me when I was a young producer.

I would sit in the middle of crowds at film festivals, and even though our work had already been judged to be very good, I would be riddled with insecurity. I can remember sitting at the Banff Television Festival several years ago, where I was appearing on a panel. There was a large crowd, numbering in the hundreds of people, waiting to hear us speak. I was filled with dread and a sense that I didn't belong there. I hadn't done enough. I didn't deserve to be on the podium.

Then, as my mind calmed down and I glanced around, I noticed that there might have been a half-dozen people in the room that had done as much or more than me. I had written, produced, executive produced or acted as a creative consultant on over one hundred and thirty television series, documentary productions or scripted episodes. In addition, I had major feature film credits, taught at two universities and won teaching award, and yet somehow, I imagined that all these people were better than I was. Now, I didn't go off on an ego trip about it. I just recognized how my mind lies to me. I was as talented as most of the people in that room. My track record spoke for itself.

I am also arrogant at times. I feel superior to others, until I meet someone more successful than I am, and then I revert to insecurity. sometimes try to be the center of attention. speak and act so I will be noticed. I try and impress others, because it makes me feel better to think I'm someone special, and I want you to know, too. I'm grateful to say that most of those traits have slowly decreased over the years, but they did plague me when I was younger. It's very embarrassing now to think back on what an obnoxious young man I was at times. What was at the root of it? Fear and insecurity.

Here are the symptoms of codependency My good feelings about who I am stem from being liked by you. My good feelings about who I am stem from receiving approval from you. Your struggles affect my serenity. My mental attention focuses on solving your problems, on relieving your pain. My attention is focused on pleasing you. My attention is focused on protecting you My attention is focused on manipulating you to 'do it my way.' Relieving your pain bolsters my self-esteem. My own hobbies and interests are put aside in favor of sharing your interests and hobbies.

Because I feel you are a reflection of me, I want your behavior and personal appearance to be dictated by my desires. I am aware of what you feel and want, rather than of what I feel and want. Even when I am not truly aware, I assume that I am. The dreams I have for my future are linked to you. My fear of rejection determines what I say and do. My fear of anger determines what I say and do. I use giving as a way of feeling safe in our relationship. My social circle diminishes as I involve myself with you. I put my values aside in order to connect with you. I value your opinion and way of doing things more than my own. The quality of life varies in relation to the quality of yours.

It's never quite as simple as it sounds. Anger is the outward manifestation of my old thinking. Many times in life, we suppress anger. That can turn into depression. Or we take it out on the wrong people, or on an unsuspecting person who happens to be the hapless victim of our unexpressed rage.

I believe the cause of these feelings for me was coming out of such a chaotic home. I had to have order. It represented manageability to me. The feelings that get triggered in me are resentment, self-pity, jealousy, prejudice, depression and physical illness.

When I get angry, I pout. I become aggressive and yell. I get agitated when I'm driving. I find myself suffering from road rage. A home or at work, I withdraw and I begin to act like a kid. Why? Because that's the learned mode I'm operating from. When these feelings surface they make no sense at all to an adult. That's because my frightened six-year-old emotional self has wrestled control of my emotions from my adult, rational, conscious mind.

Chronic infantile omnipotence has taken over. Metaphorically, I lie on the floor, kicking and screaming until I get my own way. Works when you're six. Not at thirty-six, forty-six or, God forbid, sixty-six. Of course our unconscious is not stupid. It finds wonderful ways to mask the process so we don't look quite so immature.

We cover it in a blanket of rationalization It's your fault. Not mine. And I'm only too glad to help you by pointing out your deficiencies, so you can grow as a person. I'm just justifying my point of view.

At the root of these feelings are insecurity, anxiety and resentment. What is at risk is our self-esteem, our goals, or our personal or sexual relations.

What is important for us to do is to learn

how to appropriately express our anger. When we feel like kicking the dog, slamming a door or yelling at one of the kids or our partner, we have to cool down, calm down and simply say, "I feel angry and upset." Nobody can argue with our feelings. It's not up for discussion. But they also have the right to defend their actions, and we had better be prepared to hear what they have to say. We may not like it one bit. Nevertheless, their feelings are as legitimate as mine. They may have another point-of-view that is just as valid.

What generally triggers me is the fear that I won't get what I want, or I will lose something I already have. That pushes me over the edge. If we're reducing our spending, I can't drive a new German sports car. Now I have a nice German car. But it's not a convertible. Much more economical, less pollution, but my ego does handstands because I don't have my toys anymore.

I can't emphasize this enough. I really have to treat my ego and the voice in my head that quite frankly, never shuts up as if it's a third person. What voice you are asking? Take thirty seconds of silence right now. Just stop reading and sit there for the next thirty seconds.

Have you done it? It's the one saying, "I

don't hear anything." Or, "This guy is a flake. Ge a Wayne Dyer Book, he's better."

Otherwise, it just runs the living hell out o me, and is soon joined by a whole board o directors in my head that loves to add their two cents. Especially around 4 a.m.

Our minds say we won't have enough money, so we want to hoard it. Instead of realizing that we have talents and abilities, We can earn a reasonable living, but we still go into a panic. We think we will never make another dime again This is old, unhealthy thinking that can only be replaced when we let go absolutely and trust that we will be guided in all departments of our life.

Further means of trying to control include overreacting to change. As a child, I had little control over the behavior of my father, or the things that happened in our home. As I grew older, I tried to control the feelings and behavior of others. This exemplifies itself in interpersona relations when I have to do everything myself because no one will do it as well as I will.

That only leads to passive-aggressive behavior from others who become fed up with trying to be controlled. They resent it. Or they have such a sick need to be 'saved, fixed, taken care of' that we generally end up getting rid o them because they drive us crazy with all of their needs. They become emotional vampires. We are like magnets that attract needy people. Or, like a magnet, which has a polar opposite, we repel healthy people with our unhealthy behavior.

We also demonstrate rigid behavior. There is no room for spontaneity—we become extremely upset when any of our plans are interrupted. We worry about being late. We become inflexible in our dealings with others in planning social or work events. This in turn creates stress and anxiety in our friends, partners and work associates. Compromise is a deadly disease to this way of thinking.

I would go to great lengths to manage how others saw me. I had a fear of "looking bad." The main mantra of my mother when I was a child was, "What will the neighbors think?"

Well, quite frankly, I don't give a damn anymore. I had a chance to talk to my mother before she died. When she was eighty years old, I invited her to take a workshop with me.

It was very valuable. I was able to share with her how much her fear-based behavior had scarred me, because I was terrified down to my core of what others thought of me.

I did it in a very gentle way. She got it, and we were able to resolve that this was just part of the process for both of us to let go of our old beliefs.

Twenty-six weeks to the day after she completed the workshop, she stood up for the first time and thanked everyone in the room. She asked me to come over to her house later that week. At first she was as calm as could be, and then she just started crying. She admitted to me for the first time in my life that she'd carried around so much shame because she'd never been able to go to university—she wanted to be a doctor when she was a young girl in the 1920s. Her father didn't believe women should be educated. She had to run away from home and move in with the Grey Nuns in Timmins, so she could go into nursing school.

She was also angry because on many occasions she had to step in and fix mistakes young doctors had made, without ever being acknowledged for her contribution. I had no idea that she felt this way. Here I was in my mid-forties, and I'd never had a conversation with my mother anywhere close to this level. I couldn't believe how devastated she was.

She felt that it was her fault I'd ended up

an alcoholic like my father. I pointed out to her that, in my judgment, I'd inherited a condition no different than diabetes.

It wasn't her fault. It had more to do with genetics, which I'm convinced beyond any shadow of a doubt was one of the primary causes. There was no doubt I was influenced by our alcoholic home, but the fact is, once I ingested alcohol, I felt different. It was a chemical reaction. I had a physical allergy. She or my father didn't hold me down in high school when I was feeling so insecure and say, "Here, take a big slug of this, and you'll feel better." Quite the opposite! She tried in myriad ways to help me.

She then went on to tell me that she'd always wanted to be a writer, too. She'd written a story that she wanted me to read. I still have it today. Then she said, "What do you want here in the house?"

I looked around our old family home and asked her, "Why are you asking me this now?"

"I just want to get my affairs in order," she replied. "Now I can die in peace."

For the first time in almost forty years, she was free of the guilt that somehow she'd made major mistakes with my father, my brothers and sisters, and me. She was able to let go of blaming herself for our childhoods. She had contacted my two sisters and made amends to both of them. believe both my sisters appreciated tha tremendously.

It was miraculous to see. I told her to jus relax. I was just grateful to see that she was s happy.

Eight weeks later, she lapsed into a coma at Woman's College Hospital after she made m promise that I would take care of her Wes Highland terrier, Shorty. Eight weeks before he bout, she was in fair health, but she was ready tc die and really just too tired of life to go on any further.

The doctor confirmed that she was in th process of dying. I just let go and felt the loss in a very healthy, emotional way.

Being there for her those last few days o her life was the most rewarding experience of my adult life. I am so grateful that I was there, no having to control the outcome of her death. could let go absolutely. Let go and let God.

What my mother demonstrated to me wa trust. The very thing I couldn't do with my father I could do with my mother. She never let me dowr once. If something was promised, she delivered. In retrospect, I am astounded that she was able to do so much for me. I was a kid with a lot of demands growing up. How she ever met half of her undertakings is a miracle to me. Now, with children of my own, I see how difficult it must have been for her, with no support whatsoever from my father.

But trust still remains a key issue for me today. It doesn't come easily to me. I still worry about how things will turn out. I find it hard to believe that people have my best interests at heart.

Given the nature of our home growing up, why am I so surprised? But worry is a true waste of time. Study after study has demonstrated that 95 percent of what people worry about never comes to pass. It's just the chattering of our mind—the incessant need to keep revisiting worry and catastrophizing. Think of the rotisserie I mentioned earlier that just keeps spinning around; first, it's money, then my looks, my health, death, then my career, taxes—it just keeps spinning, going nowhere. That's another area where I've learned to just thank my mind for sharing.

Another element of unhealthy thinking is

intolerance. We become judgmental, overly critical of our significant other, our kids, our associates in business, and the guy who drive the bus, the waitress in the restaurant. If we are not in a healthy state of mind, our thinking takes on a strange twist.

Fear of abandonment is another old way of thinking. It wasn't until I was in my forties that was able to come to grip with this element of my life. I found it difficult to get close to people. didn't like exposing my work or my ideas to others, for fear of criticism.

Where does it stem from? Well, in my case not knowing what to think because of the insanity of my upbringing. First, apart from my Mom, had very little emotional or intellectual encouragement.

Being so much younger than my brothers and sisters, I was like an only child to a large degree. In truth, I was probably a pain in the rea to my brothers and sisters. I was never told I had any ability by any of my teachers, or that I was ever good at anything. I had no support for any of my talents. I had to learn how to self-actualize at a very young age.

Those feelings were amplified because never knew who was going to come through the door when I was a child. It was awful waiting to see what kind of shape my father was going to be in. Then, when my mother moved us to Toronto, I just felt this incredible loss of identity and connection to home. I realize today that I was totally numb. I missed my father a great deal in those first two years. I was grateful that my mother let me call him occasionally. Invariably, he had nothing to say to me. He would inevitably be drunk when I called him, and I realized he'd totally abandoned us and me as his child.

When I was young, I tried everything at first to please him. I wanted peace in our house. As his alcoholism progressed, my interventions became more and more meaningless to him.

His initial abandonment was emotional; then it was followed by his physical departure from our lives. Given the choice, my father chose to move into the Empire Hotel in Timmins, so he could drink himself to death, undisturbed, instead of seeking help to overcome his alcoholism and retain his family.

That was the ultimate abandonment. Yet, when I stood at the same crossroads years later, I was able to make the opposite choice. That to me is a miracle.

In later years, this trait manifested itself in

me picking people that would abandon me in relationships. First, it was in business, and then in my emotional and romantic life. In romantic relationships, I was filled with insecurity. I would start off by being a caretaker, trying to fix things. If you felt bad, it was my fault. I couldn't just let you have a bad day. I would try to fix it.

This is why I desperately wanted money. I thought, if I am rich, then I don't need anyone. I will be all right on my own. It also caused me to be standoffish with people. They thought I was arrogant. I wasn't. I was afraid. It's why, when I walked into a roomful of strangers, I was terrified, and I would position myself off in a corner.

My second choice was to go get loaded, so I could walk over to a young lady and be funny. It's why high school and university were so difficult.

I actually yearned to get close to people, but the very walls I'd constructed as a child to survive, that were like a reinforced bunker to stop the pain, now became my prison. I couldn't get out, and no one could get in.

When I stood up for myself, I was filled with shame and guilt. I didn't feel I was worthy. The problem must be mine. I was loyal to a fault, and on several occasions, it came back to haunt me. I now believe I'm over it—hopefully. It gets really boring after a while. Once again, what's at the root of it? Pride and low self-esteem are the primary culprits.

So, the way we overcome it is to trust in our Higher Power. When we do that, our self-esteem increases. We are then able to let go of our need to keep acting out these unhealthy behaviors. We are able to find people who will be there for us when we need them. That is the single greatest gift I've received over these past thirty years. Today I have people I can totally trust. They are there for me through thick and thin. It is also imperative for me to let go and trust, so I can outgrow my need for abandonment. People do leave for a variety of reasons. People and circumstances change as do some relationships.

WE MUST LET GO OF THE FEAR, OR IT WILL KEEP US LOCKED INTO THIS UNHEALTHY BEHAVIOR. FEAR, LIKE RESENTMENT, IS AS FATAL AS CANCER. IT WILL EAT AWAY AT OUR LIVES UNTIL WE ARE SIMPLY SHADOWS OF OURSELVES. WHEN WE CONFRONT FEAR HEAD-ON, IT DISSIPATES EVERY TIME. FRANKLIN D. ROOSEVELT SAID IT BEST: "WE HAVE NOTHING TO FEAR BUT FEAR ITSELF."

14. I DECIDE TO BE CHANGED – STEP 4

I make decisions to surrender my will and my life to the Master Mind; I ask to be changed at depth.

Fifteen years ago I had a serious reversal in business. Unlike the old days, I didn't let it fester. I was able to express how I felt about the situation to friends, family, and my Master Mind partners. At first I was filled with rage and resentment against the two parties involved. I did have legitimate reasons to be upset. I walked out of the company and gave my power away. I should have sought legal advice. Another live and learn experience.

So, where had I been wrong? I asked myself. Was this the first time I'd ended up on the losing side of a business deal? No! Then why now? Why was I feeling everything I was feeling? As I began to take a serious look at where had I been flawed in my thinking and what I'd done—an inventory of my part in it, a pattern began to emerge.

I was overly open in my dealings with one

of my associates.

But what was really at the source of how I felt? When I went to my spiritual adviser and sought his help, we began to look at what I was feeling. I felt betrayed. I felt hurt. I felt that my contribution was not acknowledged and that I was becoming the scapegoat for another person's grave problems.

In a very unhealthy way, the blame had been shifted over to me for another's deceitful actions. This time, I was able to remove myself from the situation, although it created serious financial loss and uncertainty in my life. Nevertheless, I kept my integrity.

Coincidentally, I've ended up with something I've always dreamt of a house in the country. Have we gone hungry? No. Do I still feel the anger I did? By and large, it is gone. In fact, today I am feeling more peaceful than I ever have at any time in my life. Occasionally I will think about how the situation ended up and, depending on my mood, I might begin to contemplate the sadness I feel in the circumstances. But, I can accept the state of affairs as exactly the way they are supposed to be.

When I made the decision to leave the company I'd founded, and to sell our family home

that I'd been raised in, I was very apprehensive
What would I do to earn a living?

I was too young to retire. How could w
survive? Would we actually like living so far awa
from a major metropolitan center?

We were heading to the country—far awa
from the center of my industry, but Deb and
wanted to see if we could make a change, a
significant change in our lives. I knew that if w
didn't do it, then we never would. Our two kid
were eleven and twelve, and we knew if we put i
off, we wouldn't be able to do it once they hit thei
teens. It wouldn't have been fair to them. Plus, w
decided we would give it two years, and if w
hated it, we could always move back to the city.

So here was a case of confronting ol
thinking—unhealthy thinking—and saying, "I'm
not going to do what I've always done." I wasn'
going to stay and get into litigation and crazy
name-calling, which is what might have
happened if I'd stayed in our old neighborhood.
would try something different this time. I made
the decision to surrender my will and my life to
God, as I understood God at that time. I made the
decision to pursue an idea I'd been talking abou
for over twenty years. I would see if I could write
a book about my experiences growing up.

When we ask to be changed, at depth we are heading into new territory. I must confess that it is frightening and very uncomfortable. I knew that I couldn't stay with the company any longer, because it was an emotionally unhealthy situation for me to be there.

I can't afford emotionally unhealthy people in my life today. It doesn't mean that my former friend can't find a solution to his dilemma, and we can't be friends again, either. I believe in God's world; all things are possible

But, for today, I need to keep my distance. When I see either one, which I do, I can be civil, say hello, wish them the best and mean it, and then move on. Here is one of the most valuable lessons I've had to learn: I can't afford resentment. The analogy is; I drink poison and sit around and wait for the other guy to die.

Resentment will kill us. You may think I'm being over-dramatic. I'm not. How many heart attacks, how many murders, how many lives have been ruined because of perceived wrongs others have done us, and our inability to forgive, forget and move on? Think of the effects of resentment in the case of the hockey father here in Ontario, who killed another father a few years ago because of his resentment.

When we have a Master Mind Group, or another support group we can help others and ourselves to a healthy way. We will discover that life does work out. It does get better, and we do feel at peace again.

It was extremely difficult making the decision to leave my company and getting to a place of forgiveness and release. I went through a period of whining about it, blaming and shaming before I got to acceptance. Acceptance is the answer to all my problems. It really is. When I try to avoid pain—particularly the pain of change—stay locked into self-destructive behavior longer than it is necessary. When I can accept that change is needed and just embrace it, I begin to move through the process of healing and forgiving myself, and others, much faster. I can get over the sleepless nights, the constant replaying of the situation in my mind. I should have if only I'd...those bastards. It goes on and on, and I don't find a solution.

I had to be changed at depth and to undergo a personal transformation. If I hadn't made the decision to leave my old company, I wouldn't be sitting here today, writing this book. I wouldn't be glancing out my window at the beautiful English Bay and spending the time I am in Vancouver, which is a whole other story from my book Aging With Dignity, Living With Grace.

When I initially wanted to release this book, I never had the chance to do any marketing on it, and it needed to be edited and rewritten because so many things had changed in my life.

What I know today is I wouldn't be working out three days at week at the great pool where I do. I wouldn't feel the gratitude I do for my life today. I wouldn't have taught at a beautiful university in Vancouver last year.

No, instead I would be filled with rage and resentment at having to supplicate my desires because I was afraid to give up a paycheck. I would hate myself for being a coward. I would hate myself because I hadn't had the courage to stick up for what I knew was right. That was a major learning experience for me. When I believe in a Higher Power and trust I will be taken care of; I can move on with my life and change the way I see things.

By the way, the time has proven me right, too. The partner that had created the difficulties was removed from the company and is today hopefully doing better after years of struggling. It's my sincere hope that he can find a solution to all his challenges and problems.

I don't care, to the degree I once did, wha people think of me today. I thank both my forme partners for being great teachers. I have learned so much about human behavior, and myself, from the experience of letting go and trusting it would all work out. And, if I were ever to realize I was in the wrong, I could go to them and acknowledge it too. That to me is one of the greatest gifts I've eve received in my life.

What I find particularly interesting, is tha this situation is identical to ones I created many years ago, only the tables had been totally reversed on me this time. I also got to see that I'c finally cleaned the Karmic slate. I am now free o old thinking and acting, the majority of the time.

I am free. Free to pursue a new way of life a new way of thinking—one that allows me tc recognize that my old thinking was harmful to my health, both physically and psychologically.

So, when we turn our will and life over to a Higher Power of our choice and ask to be changec at depth, what does that look like in practica terms? Do we sit under the Bodhi Tree waiting for a message? I don't think so. Part of my malady was trying to control. I felt that, if I were not in control, then I was heading toward some catastrophic experience.

We begin by just making a decision. We decide that doing it our way has not worked. It may have produced certain positive results.

I was quite successful at getting projects accomplished. I was successful raising money. I did have some truly amazing parties, which I will be grateful for until the day I die. But I was unsuccessful holding onto anything.

Further, the price I paid for my accomplishments—the cost emotionally and physically—was exceptionally high.

As I wrote earlier, there was no peace of mind. No sense of accomplishment. There was no sense of community.

I seldom had anyone to share any of my great moments with. Conversely, over the past 30 years I have enjoyed the success I've had. First as a father to my two youngest children Brendan and Laurel. I was a Scout Leader. By and large, I have the same people working with me today that I started with 35 years ago. While not everyone will ever like us, I can tell you the majority of the people I've worked with in Film and Television as well as teaching like me, and I like them. So the whole experience of my early career up until 1987 has been completely transformed as a result of letting go of old ideas and being willing to change.

But, I had to let go of old ideas completely When I stopped drinking at twenty-two years c age, all I did was stop drinking. I didn't chang any parts of my personality. I was unwilling t surrender to the concept of a Higher Power. I wa unwilling to give up my character flaws tha plagued me. I was totally unwilling to trust tha God would guide me. Instead, I only called upor God when I was in serious trouble. I expected Hin to become a pitch hitter for me, but, I was t discover, that's not how God operates.

When I made the decision to change, i posed a very serious moral dilemma for me. First I imagined that I would stop having to be cool Now let me assure you, cool was more a figmen of my imagination than reality.

While I was fairly cool in my dress, my attitude, and my outlook were as conservative a could be—and I successfully hid it from really cool people. I was a phony cool. I was s traditional, so conservative, that it hurt. Dee down, I shocked myself with my actions.

My second big moral dilemma had to do with my fear that I would end up a religious whacko—especially the kind I did not hold in high regard. I thought, if I decide to turn my will and life over to the care of God, then I'm going to have to stand on the street corner and sing for my supper. I also had a vision of me screaming, "The end is nigh."

I don't mean to denigrate the work of those who do this. I just wouldn't have the courage of conviction that they do. I identified more with Monty Python's Life of Brian than I did with mainstream religion. I can't tell you how afraid I was that this was going to happen to me.

So, I began taking small steps. I was willing to surrender my anger. That was causing me tremendous difficulties at home. I remember yelling at my young son, Brendan, one morning when he was about three or four, and he started to cower.

He was terrified of me. There I was my father again, and this time, I had no alcohol or drugs as an excuse. It shocked me that I could be this way. I had to surrender to this character defect.

By the way, that son, who is now 26, worked with me for a few years, and I think we've had one harsh word in that period. We change! That's the good news.

Making the decision to give up anger was

an interesting experience. The more I prayed to have my anger removed, the more often I became angry. I was stuck behind idiots that couldn' drive. I had people giving me the finger in traffic My ex-wife seemed to be more difficult. The kid were acting up more than ever, and I felt like Sisyphus in the Greek myth who pushes the boulder up to the top of the mountain, only to have it roll right back down again. The more committed I was to having anger removed, the more opportunities and situations involving anger kept coming up.

I asked to have fear removed. The momen I did that, I was confronted by situations that created significant amounts of terror. First was fear of financial insecurity. I have been self employed my whole life—with the exception o teaching at three universities, which I did for almost ten years.

I've always had to fend for myself. I couldn' reconcile how it would be okay for me to turn my business and financial life over to some kind o Higher Power, but here I was in a constant state of dread about our financial future.

A Higher Power might be okay at things spiritual, but how about a profit-and-loss statement? How about a business plan? What about sales? Being a producer is this generation's version of being a traveling sales executive. I go to one of the Meccas of entertainment—Los Angeles, New York, Cannes or London. I have my bag of goodies: a script, a commitment from a director, perhaps a star attached, a deal with a Canadian broadcaster and a European one. I do a little dog-and-pony show for some poor executive that has as much interest in hearing what I have to say as he/she does in getting hemorrhoids because it's just another pitch.

The only difference between me and the countless others trying to do what I do is I've done it enough times successfully that I create a horrible situation for these executives. It is a codependent's nightmare. Why? Because they're filled with anxiety because I have done it before, and this presents two dilemmas for them. First, I might have a winner, and if they say yes, and it isn't, then they could be fired, or humiliated.

Second, if they turn me down, they know I'm going across the street where they might say yes, and then when their meeting log is reviewed by the head of development and he or she realizes they turned down this project, and it was successful, then the executive might get fired.

Hollywood is the only town in the world

where you can die of encouragement. People often don't want or know how to say no, so they keep saying maybe.

One of the ongoing fears I've had is about not being able to pay off all of my creditors Initially, I was very frightened to contact them. had to change this. So beginning about twenty nine years ago, I started to call, write or visit as many as I could find.

I was very nervous and self-conscious contacting the ones who'd wanted to sue me for Dixie Lanes.

In spite of that, I sat down and started writing letters to the ones I couldn't speak to in person. I explained to them in a frank and forthright manner what had happened to me With the exception of one or two people, everyone was gracious, patient and understanding. Many offered to help again, which completely overwhelmed me. They were quite emphatic that if this was another ploy to use them, they might think about seriously hurting me, but if I was sincere, then they were willing to give me one more chance.

Not bad, considering the majority of them were lawyers, which made the threat of my premature departure from the planet rather interesting.

To change my view of money, I had to make a decision that I could no longer seek out investment money from individuals the way I once did. They would have to acknowledge that this venture was risky and sign a document acknowledging that fact.

`When I didn't do that with my investors, that was always the money that got me in trouble. My decision was only to go to the people who finance the work I do. In other words, I would only go to broadcasters or studios to fund my projects. If I went for the private money, they would have to be sophisticated investors like I have with my good friend and business partner Sonny.

I also had to look at my spending and saving patterns. Where had we gone wrong in our personal finances? We were constantly in debt and had unsecured creditors.

So, we had to stop going into debt, and we had to start watching our spending. My ex-wife Deb should get a lot of credit here, as she was the responsible one, and she created a spending plan. We began keeping track of how much money each one of us spent in a given month.

When you're not conscious of that fact, it is

unsettling how much money you can waste or inconsequential spending. I'm still using these spending plans today, and I do my weekly numbers to watch my spending.

I've noticed that discussing money when was married was probably the most difficult task we took on. I hated it. It made me totally uncomfortable. When I surrendered my finances to my Higher Power, when we were willing to be changed at depth in this area, then changes started to take place.

When Deb and I met, I was a high-flying divorcee. Without knowing anything about me she started a relationship, and we moved in together. We had a son, Brendan, within a year. My old behavior was unacceptable. I knew needed help because of all the issues out of my past. I sought out professional help.

When I prayed and asked for guidance changes began to happen. Once again, the same old pattern that had been present in my other issues, like anger, began to come to the forefront.

Deb and I suffered from what we called divorce head. Whenever we would get in one of our fights over money, one of us would say "That's it. I'm out of here. I want a divorce."

The trouble was, neither one of us wanted one at that time, but we both had patterns of running when things weren't working out. So we started to look for help. We did couple's work. We did communications training. We did marriage counseling, and all of those activities became the building blocks of a much richer and more patient, forgiving relationship and marriage.

While we did get a divorce, probably ten years after we started this process, it was not finances that were at the root of it. It was just time for us to move on, and we were able to do that in a mutually loving and supportive way, and I'm sure she would say the same thing.

In Harville Hendrix's book, Getting the Love You Want, he points out some very simple exercises that I find are good to do.

Do something nice for your partner. Whether it's helping clean up after dinner, doing the laundry once a week or just saying, "I love you." Those are all small but important things that anyone of us can do to strengthen a relationship.

When we ask to be changed at depth, we are asking to for help to do some very heavy and dramatic work. I'm clear that, whenever I want to change, all the forces of nature and my unconscious go to work, trying to get me to undo that decision.

Change is hard. Change is challenging Being changed at depth is damn nearly impossible, unless you do have the help of a Higher Power or God.

One of the essential ingredients of the Master Mind principles is to belong to a Master Mind Group. I had one in Toronto almost twenty years ago, and I'm now doing one in Vancouver with several friends.

I had a second Master Mind Group in Kingston, near where my country house is. I met weekly with my friend Richard and one friend Bill, who was a retired psychiatrist. Bill died a few years ago and was an avowed agnostic, and he was the man who convinced me pray for the peace of mind and humility. I will be forever grateful to Bill.

My original Master Mind group had five men. What we have in common is our desire to change and be changed at depth. Today there are 6 of us, and we have three women and three men.

It is important for me to have like-minded people because God uses these people: when two or more are gathered, then I am there too. If a

Master Mind Group is not available, then as I mentioned earlier there are numerous self-help or 12-Step Groups including Alanon, Adult Children of Alcoholics or Codependents Anonymous that can provide the support you need. It is in this environment where you can utilize the support of others to change.

I want to emphasize again—it is God as you understand God to be. There is no theology involved here. You do not have to believe in my idea of who God is or anyone else's.

Today, my Higher Power is my best friend who I can just talk to like I would a friend and I've let got of my childhood Catholic beliefs. And I have no issue with the Catholic Church personally.

We support one another in achieving our goals of transforming our lives and finding a new way of life. We can be open and honest and share very intimate and personal details of our life because we trust these people. It is imperative to find others who share your beliefs. It not only helps in a practical way, but in ways we can't see at first, it gives us suppor

There is strength in numbers, especially in the area of spirituality. In time, we also receive the benefit and blessings of being able to help others.

It is important to read spiritual material to help us change. We need to feed our mind as we feed our body. If we don't take the time to nurture our intellect and emotions, then will suffer from spiritual malnutrition.

It is necessary for us to keep constantly looking for whatever inspirational materials are out there. Whether it is listening to tapes by Marianne Williamson or reading her books or listening to Jack Boland's tapes, I have grown tremendously.

Whether it's reading Deepak Chopra Harville Hendrix, Scott Peck's The Road Less Traveled or reading the Bible; we have to give our souls sustenance.

After mocking him for years, I read Eckart Tolle's books, and I was pleasantly surprised. In truth, I was just jealous of him.

I believe it is good for all of us to visit alternative faiths to help us understand one another. What becomes abundantly evident in a short time is how much they all have in common, not how different they are.

I think I loved Unity because their theology

is so inclusive. At the Unity, I attend they have a motto: "One God, Many Paths."

If a church is not for you and you are serious about change, then there are many spiritual fellowships that may meet in a church but have no religious affiliation. You may be suffering from any one of the dozens of addictions and maladies that are treated by the various twelve-step programs. All of those technologies of transformations have the same goal: to help anyone undergo significant and lasting personality change at depth.

15. I FORGIVE – STEP FIVE

I forgive myself for all my mistakes and shortcomings. I also forgive all other persons who may have harmed me. I ask for Forgiveness Too.

When I started writing this book, I was acutely aware that I needed to forgive myself for some horrendous mistakes I had made early in my life. There were also many people in my life had to forgive. I had to forgive myself for having blown one of the greatest opportunities a human being could ever have in life—with my original family and my children Andrew and Colleen.

Then I had to forgive myself for completely blowing up my producing career. To this day, don't honestly know why I did what I did with my first children. It's what I thought was right at the time because I was in so much pain emotionally.

When I was twenty-four years old, I thought

I needed a new start. That's why I headed out west to start a new life.

Unfortunately, it took quite a few years for me to recognize that what I had done, as far as my children went, was a mistake. I shouldn't have left them. Period.

That is one of the facts I have to accept today and forgive myself for moving to Vancouver. It is the only regret I have.

When I was thirty-five years old, I was at the zenith of my professional career, but my personal life was a total disaster. We were so hot; there was nothing that should have or could have stopped me, except me. I had everything one could hope for in business. We had world recognition for our work in film. We had the respect of our peers, as well as the International Press, who nominated us for two Golden Globe awards in 1983. We had successfully raised millions of dollars for our various productions. We could essentially get a meeting with anyone we wanted to in Los Angeles in the mid to late 80s.

Then I allowed my addiction to take over. I sabotaged myself and ruined a golden opportunity. I couldn't understand why I was operating the way I was.

I couldn't or wouldn't accept that I had disease. I couldn't accept that I was allergic t anything that was mood-altering. Whateve mood-altering substance I ingest set off a patter of mental and physical craving that nothing coul control, until I accepted I was powerless an asked a Higher Power to help me.

I had to forgive my father for his action when he was drunk and assaulted my mothe and me. I had to forgive him for the horror of m childhood and the ongoing violence I lived with. had to forgive him for abandoning me as a child

I had to forgive my mother for leaving m alone with him when I was so young. I knew tha if I didn't forgive them, then there was no way could forgive myself.

As I said in the previous chapter and it i well worth repeating: anger and resentment ar analogous to terminal cancer. They will eat at u until we either kill ourselves—literally o figuratively—or those closest to us. We becom poisoned. We literally lose our lives over anothe human being. They move in and live rent-free in our heads. We cannot shake loose of the wrap that hold us in bondage to the feelings o injustice. Does it mean we sit back and allov people to continue abusing or misusing us? No

We take responsibility for our feelings, and we take constructive steps to break free of the emotions of anger, of resentment and of wanting to get even.

Earlier, I said having resentment and wanting to get even is like you drinking poison yourself, and waiting for the other person to die. It is one of the great paradoxes of life. Christ said when he was asked how many times we should forgive, seven times? He said, "Seventy times seven."

We cannot stop forgiving, regardless of how much we've been harmed. As a matter of fact, the more we have suffered, the greater the need to forgive. Why?

Because it will allow us to walk into the sunlight of the spirit and break free of the toxic feelings of shame, blame and hatred. And breaking free, like all the other steps we've looked at, is no easy task. But what are the payoffs? Peace of mind, for starters: a sense that we no longer need to focus on people's injustices to us. We can let them go and feel good about ourselves, and what a beautiful gift that is.

There is such great freedom in letting go of these negative feelings. When we do, we are overwhelmed with a sense of happiness and joy.

The fact is, when we're free of anger and resentment, it is like being reborn again.

Another important element of forgiveness i a sense of acceptance for ourselves because know I have hurt others, too. Not intentionally but Jack Boland often talks about the consciou and subconscious mind, and how they impact us

There have been a few instances in m interpersonal relationships with woman especially when I was between 27 and 35 that deeply regret. It is my hope that any of the women I was dating with during this period, when I wa not available or healthy emotionally will find it ir their hearts to forgive me. I am genuinely baffled why I did some of the things I did.

Quite often, we're not aware of why we are operating the way we do. Our actions are ofter hurtful and judgmental because that's how we've operated most of the time. In my case was a very grumpy guy a lot of the time. I didn't mean to be I just was.

If someone doesn't ask us specifically for feedback about their behavior or actions, I do no believe it is a good idea for any of us to sugges any advice.

The trouble is; we are often trying to resolve

problems with inaccurate data. What is ironic to me about the subconscious mind will help me to resolve problems.   That is, if I do ask it to help me before I go to bed at night, I say something like, "I have this problem. I don't like Harry because Harry has just cheated me out of money, or he's run off with my wife. What is my lesson? What am I to learn? Please guide me to find the right or appropriate answer."

I can assure you that the majority of the time if I continue this process over and over, I will get the right answer. It might be a hunch or intuition. Or I might find myself led to someone or an event where all of a sudden, I hear what I needed to hear to resolve the problem. There is a caveat here, however: I may not like the answer.

So, what is the first step to forgiveness? We have to be willing to pray for those who've hurt us and—here's the kicker—we have to be willing to have them obtain everything we could ever want in our life. Oh my, this is hard to do, especially when the black-hearted bastards deserve all of the possible plagues, illnesses and demons that God or nature could deliver unto them. But today, I know this is not the right prayer. With a Higher Power's help, I know I'm able to release whatever anger or resentment I feel toward him/her, and I am given the ability to forgive those I need to forgive.

As I wrote earlier, I had as good an excus as I'll ever have to hate someone I was in busines with back fifteen years ago. I had to wish thes individuals all the success in the world with th company I formed.

But, as I also noted, I ultimately handled it It took me almost six months to forgive them. couldn't sleep for several months.

And that's when I knew I had to do something constructive because I was suffering. had to start praying. I had to be willing to let then be successful and to enjoy their lives. It was so difficult because I felt possessed by negativ feelings. And what's at the root of it? Pride. Self centered pride. And underneath all of that is hur and betrayal.

I want to emphasize again when I don't ge what I want, or I lose or may lose something have; that becomes the chief activator of these negative personality traits that cripple me.

We have to be bigger than the situation What is remarkable is how, when we can do it, we start to experience real peace, real serenity. And then the big payoffs start. We can forgive ourselves for many of the mistakes we've made ir the past. While I'm not one who subscribes to Eastern religions, I do believe they contain a great deal of truth. One of the most prominent truths that they contain is the Law of Karma.

Taking responsibility for our lives and the way they turn out is very liberating. At least in the Western world, our adversaries only harm us emotionally and financially. It puts things in perspective.

When I look at the justice meted out by the Taliban in Afghanistan, or ISIS in Iraq, or the Khmer Rouge all those years ago in Southeast Asia, I shudder.

Combined, all of these regimes tortured and murdered millions of people whose points of view differed from their black or white thinking.

Once again, I have peace in my life. I have a sense that all is well in the universe, and I will end up where I am supposed to, regardless of myself. As I said, I don't know what is right for me or anyone else. It's not my job to know. It's almost like life is none of my business. In other words, when we trust my Higher Power, we don't need to know the results. We have to have the faith that it will work out, and it usually does. Never quite in the way, we would expected it to, but it does work out.

If we're not able to forgive, then we live our lives filled with poison. We are so overwhelmed by negative thinking and feelings that nothing works out. We are no fun to be around.

People walk the other way when we show up. I have nothing to give in a relationship because everything is about me. We are consumed with self. But when we can forgive, and we can let go, we are given a new lease on life. We create room for others, and we have compassion. And people like people with compassion. Compassion breeds love and respect.

One of the prayers I've used extensively from Catherine Ponder's book is (please feel free to substitute whatever name you are comfortable with): Divine Power in me is my releasing Power. Divine Power in me is my forgiving Power. Divine Power in me now frees me from all resentment or attachment toward or from people, places, or things of the past or present that are no longer part of the Divine Plan for my life. Divine Power in me manifests my perfect place with honest people and the real prosperity now.

It is truly beautiful to experience release from these feelings of anger and hurt. It gives you back your life. It allows you to wake up in the morning filled with joy again. But what about the people we've hurt? If you're human, then I suggest, regardless of how little you think you've hurt or harmed others, there will be individuals from our lifetimes that we have injured or hurt.

I know that I had to be forgiven by my family for the times I'd never shown up, or been dishonest with them about what was going on with me. It was not easy facing my brothers or sisters, and especially my firstborn children.

I've tried to explain my illness to my son, using this analogy. It's not an excuse for my behavior, but it might help him, or my daughter understand where I was—physically, emotionally and spiritually.

How would you feel if someone had a rare form of a brain tumor or mental illness, and their actions were reprehensible while they were sick? Would you hate them, or forgive them? Most people always say, "I'd forgive them, of course."

I suggest to you that if you are in a home with an alcoholic, drug addict, or someone suffering from the disease of addiction—whether it is gambling, sex or food, and especially food— one of the ones that I seemed to have missed, then I pray you can see these people as sick and in need of your sympathy and prayers.

We don't release them from th
responsibility of their actions or just excuse them
But what they have is an illness, recognized b
the American Medical Association.

Addiction is perhaps the most insidiou
disease known to humankind because those wh
are addicted are the architects of their adversity
They have no one to blame but themselves. Mos
live in denial about it. They think they can sto
themselves without any outside help.

Occasionally, very occasionally, som
alcoholics can, but the number is so infinitesimal
it is hardly worth mentioning. The vast majority
of alcoholics/addicts go to their grave
prematurely because they can't accept they hav
a medical condition that is not curable, but car
be arrested by total abstinence.

When it came to my creditors, I felt tota
embarrassment. I still do at times. After Dixi
Lanes, I would receive the most abusive anc
harassing calls imaginable.

There were times when I broke down alone
and cried. I had no idea what to do. I was sc
overwhelmed by the amount of money I owed.
didn't want to owe this money. I didn'
consciously want to screw up my life. The fact is
before Dixie Lanes; I'd always paid my investors

and creditors. Once I got free of the initial trauma not once in nearly 30 years, have I replicated any of those situations.

To me, one of the greatest hurdles I've had to overcome is my selfishness. But I know if I'm to be truly forgiven and learn to forgive myself, I must continue the path of finding the right answer in this area. When I can forgive others for the harm they've done me, I am forgiven too. It allows the universe to help us out—to find a solution to our dilemmas.

What has become abundantly clear is that fundamentally, we are all the same. Yes, there will be about five percent of the population that will have their affairs in order, and will become self-sufficient regardless of what happens with the economy. The vast majority of us, however, are not that lucky. We need to find a way to forgive others and ourselves. We need to be able to work and live in harmony, or else many of us will find ourselves out on the street, cold and hungry.

It was at my Master Mind Group in Toronto and Oakville that I was able to do my original work on forgiving my business partners. Week after week, I would ask to be able to forgive them. It is so important for all of us to have someone we can talk to about these issues. My Group gave me a safe place where they wouldn't participate in gossip, but only in constructive work, so I could resolve the resentments I had and get on with my life.

Forgiveness is the key to happiness. Forgiveness is the key to a useful life. Forgiveness is essential if we are to move on in our lives. You may have been sexually abused. You need professional counseling, no matter what anyone says. Yes, God can heal it, but God also uses people to help us recover. Religion alone is not enough. Spirituality alone is not sufficient. But it is an intricate piece of the puzzle in putting our lives back together again.

Forgiveness sets us free—free from hatred, free from fear and free to love again. I suggest it is impossible to love if we have resentment in our lives. It's just not possible. God loves us regardless of what we've done. Too bad we don't like ourselves so easily. Self-forgiveness is the greatest gift you can give yourself.

16. I ASK – STEP SIX

I make known my specific request, asking my partner's support, in knowing that the Higher Mind is fulfilling my needs.

By now, it should be apparent to you that the best way to work these steps is with one or more people. I read in the literature and heard in his tapes that Jack had many Master Mind partners. It's okay to have more than one Master Mind group, in his opinion. One might be with your spouse or significant other. One might be with your kids. One might be like the one I have here in Vancouver, or the one I still have near my home in Ontario.

I have also participated in an online Master Mind Group, who are primarily in the United States. They are wonderful people, and each week as we put our requests out there, they respond with love, wisdom, and kindness. That group is split evenly between men and women. Possibly you can find people at any number of self-help groups that I've mentioned previously.

You can state your purpose in the Maste
Mind Groups and ask for guidance and prayer t
help you achieve whatever it is you wish to create
Whether it's to help you develop a deeper, mor
meaningful marriage or relationship or to guid
you in matters of business or spirituality, it work
best if we're working it with someone else.

When I forget to ask for help in m
relationship, or when I think I can do it on m
own, that's when I get into trouble. It's not a wis
move on my part. When I let my mind take over
I'm almost always guaranteed not to produce th
results I want. I have a mind that should have
little sign on it: "Dangerous neighborhood. Do no
enter alone. Watch for falling toxic ideas."

The other significant area I find a challeng
(which would be any time it comes up) is money
As I wrote earlier, budgeting, spending, saving
having or not having, are all hot buttons for me
There was a time before I sought spiritual hel
when I would go completely crazy in my thinking
That would last about an hour, and then I woul
start to think, "Hold on.

What is the one common denominator tha
is present in all my financial issues? Me!" Thi
question led me to begin investigating why I ha

the attitude I did about money. It was, in my opinion, a learned behavior. My father was my role model, and not a good one.

However, my mother turned her life around, and I began to investigate what can I do to change my attitude about money.

I have a plan to repay my creditors. And I try not to use unsecured credit today, although that changed on January 4, 2010, when a young man assaulted me, and I ended up with a severe brain injury. I am still fighting my way back from that experience.

Today I keep track of my spending, and I keep track of my numbers. I have not had a financial crisis in over twenty years. When I am conscious, when I ask for help and guidance with my finances and ask for solvency, I am led to the best possible outcome.

After my divorce, I thought no more relationships. We will have to see how that works out. I've tried once more seriously, but my heart got broken. Damn, I hate that. However, I did know I was alive, and if the right woman came along tomorrow, I'd probably be prepared to dive in one more time. After all, if you don't succeed the first or second time, well, try, try again.

One of the best decisions that I've eve
made was to move to the country fifteen year
ago. When I was married, we talked about it fo
over ten years. Now I wonder, what took us s
long? Before I started Master Minding, I used th
concept of 'picturing,' which works well with th
Master Mind principle.

I put pictures on a large sheet of Bristo
board. About three years ago, I cut out photos c
the Pacific Ocean and a view overlooking th
water. Today, I have that view in Vancouver, an
I still have my house in the country in Ontario
which I am now trying to sell. That house was m
original goal about fifteen years ago.

Now I have a picture of both Vancouver an
Toronto. I want a nice apartment in Toronto tha
I can be at a minimum of one week a month fo
either my production company or for my writin
and speaking. I am in the middle of trying t
decide, do I let go of my production company an
focus on writing and speaking and teaching. I'v
applied to another university here in Vancouver
I love teaching. Three of my four children and tw
of my four grandkids are in Toronto. My oldes
daughter who just wrote me yesterday is ir
Franklin Tennessee, just outside Nashville.
have pictures up for all my children an
grandkids and the affirmation that I can spenc

time with all of my kids and grandchildren. I have my picture in the middle of all my children and grandchildren.

Seeing what you want, being crystal clear about what you want can help the process of obtaining whatever it is you desire out of life. If you want a car, get a brochure of that car and place it on your Bristol board. It is a private matter, and it is between you, your Higher Power and your group partners.

Don't take it out to show it to your friends. They make think you've lost your mind, but trust me: you'll have found it.

I have a picture up of a 1964 Corvette Stingray convertible. I would just love one. I have a picture up of a 34 foot Catalina Sailboat. A part of me would love to have it in San Diego in the winter and Vancouver in the summer. A tad expensive, but let's see what God can do with that request. I am open to all possibilities.

Do you want good health? Put a picture up of when you were healthy and ask for it. Write out an affirmation that God is supplying you with perfect health, wealth, and understanding then brings your request to your partners. Do you want to travel to exotic locations? Get a travel brochure and have your destination up on the board, too

When I write out my goals and put them o:
board, and then bring them to my Master Min
partners, I accomplish most of them.

This year, I'm going after my big ones.
want this book and Aging With Dignity, Livin
With Grace to both be Best Sellers.   That is, i
will generate talks and revenue for me that wi:
help pay off the last of the creditors from that $·
million of debt, which is now less than tw
hundred thousand dollars. But I have to b
specific.

Does it have to be a widespread literar,
success? No. If people buy it as an eBook and fin·
it useful, then it is a success. If one person ou
there   can   utilize   something   I've   learne·
somewhere else, and it helps them, then this bool
is a success. If I can pay off some, all, or th·
majority of my original creditors, then this bool
is a real success. It will be a matter of degrees o
success. I will write on a piece of paper and hav·
it beside a picture of me with the words: "Deb
free and happy." I have received 39, five out o
five-star reviews on Aging With Dignity, Livin
with Grace.   I have just asked one of the mos
successful companies in the book marketin
world to help me. Let's see what comes of that.

You may want a new career so you can be self-supporting. Put whatever it is you want on paper, and then declare it to your Master Mind partner/s. It helps to be very specific. Then, let go of the results. I will expand on this point in the next chapter.

Here, I have to take into account that whatever I desire must also be in my best interests for the greatest good for all involved. If I want something that will create a negative result, then chances are it's not going to work. If we hate someone, and we ask our Master Mind to get him/her for us, then it's not going to work. Or, we may want to beat someone out in business because of ego.

Chances are, that's not going to work. If we want to steal someone's girlfriend or wife, it is not likely to happen. So we must be aware of what it is we are asking for, and how it might be of value to those around us, too. Our requests are to be for our greatest good, and as I said, I often don't know what is good for you or me. So I trust my higher power only to create situations where I can learn and benefit others. This or something better, God, let thy will be done.

I do love my nice apartment in Vancouver. I sit each morning, coffee in hand, appreciating the incredible view of English Bay, the ship moored in the Bay, the North Shore Mountains. love my daily inspirational books, my journal, and I spend at least an hour a day getting ready to meet the world. I am so blessed.

I am trying to be a good friend and a good father today. I would like to find the right person to share my life with, and I will let go of that request and not try and force it.

When I think about what I can contribute to my family and friends and try and share the load fifty-fifty and don't walk around in a constant state of expectancy, it's amazing how good life is. Old ideas die hard, slow, painful deaths.

Quite often, people's minds will automatically go to a default setting, just like a computer. When I think about giving up my production company here is where my mind goes "I'll be busted and disgusted."

The fact is, whenever I've prayed for guidance and asked for help, it's always been fine so far. In my case, when I originally moved to the country from Toronto, I was able to keep working as a writer, producer. Our kids don't have scurvy or rickets. We had gas in the cars and hey, I still have a nice car that is paid off. The lights are still on, as is the heat. I'm doing pretty well, I think. I am under some financial distress today as I've used a significant portion of my savings to come out to Vancouver to be treated for my brain injury, but the recovery from that has been miraculous.

Will I ever be able to produce again? I honestly don't know, but I've now gone over 335 no's, and I'm thinking it is time to call it a day and accept that my career as I knew if before I was assaulted is over.

So far, I've been able to stay alive, first by teaching last year, and I've had two small series ideas approved, and I've been writing and developing these two ideas.

Do I have everything I want? No, but in tough times like last year, I was able to utilize some of my savings because I had made changes over a decade ago. I put away a reasonable amount of money for my retirement.

It helps to have a partner who shares your belief so that we can take chances in life. Too many people are afraid to step out in faith and try anything. We're only here once—you might as well go for the gusto.

Live for today, and live as if it is your last

day on earth. One of these days, it will be, and w might as well get as much living in as we can. W don't have a lot of time to waste here on earth The whole economic meltdown of the last fev years has eviscerated people's pensions a companies like Nortel where employees though they would have it all. Same with aut manufacturing.

There are no guarantees in life except tha we will all face difficulties at some point in ou lives.

I believe if we try to be of service in ou occupations and ask for guidance, we will b taken care of somehow. In thirty years of bein; self-employed, I've never missed a meal. Yes, I'v had financial difficulties. However, we got helj with financial planning.

You would be well served to have a simpl business plan or a spending plan. Regardless o how simple it is, you should have stated goal: that are written out. It is a good idea to keep traci of your spending and earnings. You will never go broke if you have more coming in than going out But, ensure you have money set aside for yoursel every two weeks.

It's important as well to be able to take time off and give yourself important necessities: <

holiday every year and some basic luxuries, like entertainment, travel, a car or now with car shares a chance to drive one for a few hours to visit friends.

I've right sized into a small one-bedroom apartment, but it is still a nice home.

I've never ended up on the street. I find that our needs were always met when we are right with the universe. Not all of my wants, but a lot of them. And never quite in the way I expected them to be met.

With my current Master Mind group, we get together once a week to a Community Center. Originally, my group met in homes when we were doing it in Toronto and Oakville. In Kingston and early on in Vancouver, we met in restaurants and coffee shops. But in Vancouver, we all head to one central location.

In Kingston, we were lucky enough to find an Anglican(Episcopalian) church where they were very supportive of our idea. We all threw a few dollars into the hat each week, and we gave it to the church. You might want to start it out that way.

Every week, anywhere from two to six of us meet, with five to ten minutes each to share about our week. Then we ask for what it is we need o desire. We all have families. We all have career or new business opportunities. We pray for th peace of mind, humility, clarity of thought, anc guidance in all our business affairs.

We all wish to be successful in ou endeavors. We all wish to be more connected tc our Higher Power. We all want to be bette partners, husbands, fathers, brothers, anc members of society.

In my case, I am desirous of a new caree where I can be of service to others if I can nc longer produce film or television. That migh mean inspirational speaking, wherever anc whenever I get the chance. I know I enjoy meetin people, and have a gift for speaking. The challenge for me is to trust that my prayer is being answered. I've been asking for almost ter years for this change.

I find that I feel somewhat conflicted abou asking God for things. I worry I am too selfish. I was told that it would be best if I only prayed for God's will. Part of my healing process has beer for me to realize it is okay to ask God for help. I want to get closer to God's will, with my career choices. I want help to raise the necessary funds to pay off all of my old creditors. I want to earn enough to meet my needs so I can live comfortably.

It is also okay to ask a Higher Power to help us with our projects. I want to help. I want guidance. I want prosperity. Today, though, I've learned that success means so much more than just money. I want to experience the fullness of life's riches. I want to travel with someone special, so we can see the wonders I've seen. I want to experience spiritual riches, and I do that by trying to be of service.

I want to try and help wherever I can, with little regard for the benefit. If I give of my time, I find myself with more time. If I give money, I seem blessed with more money. If I give to the hungry or help a friend back on his or her feet, I'm helped in return. If I want to keep something, something I value, then the best thing I can do is give it away. Paradoxical but true!

One of the prayers and affirmations I use today is: I am worthy, and I deserve a happy and peaceful relationship and family life. We deserve a nice home, sufficient revenues to meet our needs, and a successful career. I deserve God's love and generosity.

Every part of me used to experience discomfort when I would say that affirmation. I

did not feel worthy when I first started. I did no
feel I deserved God's love or any blessings. But
have changed. Today, it is okay for me to ask God
to help me resolve difficulties in my relationships
It is good to ask for help with forgiveness. It i:
good to ask our Higher Power, God, to bles:
others. I have often prayed for all those who los
their lives in the World Trade Center, the Tsunam
a few years ago in Asia, the earthquake in Japan
I also asked that God bless the families and the
children. "Please give them Peace" has been my
prayer. I have done the same for all the othe:
natural and man-made disasters. I canno
understand these events as they are part of the
mystery of life.

It is very powerful to have partners with
whom we can share our longings. When two o:
more are gathered, there is a shift in one's
consciousness. It is apparent that something
quite remarkable is happening.

There have been recent studies done or
cancer patients who've been prayed for by others
for healing. It doesn't matter whether they know
it or not, according to this study. Those who've
been prayed for experience remissions more
readily than those who haven't.

There is empirical proof that praying works

Having Master Mind partners, who pray with us and join us in empowering our requests, is a wonderful experience. It is right and good to be healed of childhood trauma. It is right and good to ask to be able to let go of the power of the past to haunt us and to be freed from the pain and agony that we experienced as children. That is what I believe both God and the universe want for us. We are worthy human beings.

I believe the more our prayers and requests are rooted in the spiritual; the more likely they are to be answered expediently.

For many of us who came out of dysfunctional families, we are often challenged by both financial and emotional success. We don't know how to expect it or receive it, and we often eliminate any good fortune that comes our way because we don't think we deserve it.

That is why I also believe it is all right to ask our Master Mind for material achievements. I have desires that I mentioned earlier.

I now released those requests to my Higher Power, and when the time is right, they will be manifested. I always add the phrase, "Please guide me, God, to achieve the following, if it is your will- or something better." First and foremost in my case are the necessary funds to pay off all the people I feel I have an obligation to from so long ago. Second is for peace of mind solvency and the love of my family and friends.

I believe when my requests will help others I will truly be blessed and helped. It will enable me to reach those goals in record time.

17. I GIVE THANKS – STEP SEVEN

I Give Thanks: I give thanks that the Master Mind is responding to my needs, and assume the same feelings I would have if my request were already fulfilled.

The one way I have discovered to create more of anything in life is to give thanks for what I already have. Too often, people believe they have nothing. All it would take for any Canadian, American or Western European to realize how fortunate we are is to travel to some parts of the world where they have nothing. Children are dying by the hundreds every minute of every day in parts of Africa. People live in grinding poverty in India.

Children are sold into prostitution to give the family money in parts of Asia and South Asia. Life is cheap in many parts of the world. It was not too long ago that children were murdered every day and every night in some South American countries, to get rid of the begging and stealing problem. Murdered!

It is beyond comprehension to me that thi
goes on in so-called civilized countries, but i
does.

When I think of how we perceive childre
here in North America, it is mind-boggling tha
society as a whole allows these actions to tak
place, but it does.

That gives me pause to reflect that while
may not have a mansion, I do have a warm bed t
sleep in and enough food to eat. I do hav
plumbing to relieve myself in private, and ho
water to take a shower or bath in comfortably. T
a significant portion of the world, these ar
unheard-of luxuries. We have cars, as do larg
numbers of North Americans and Europeans
Australian's, New Zealanders and now in growing
numbers in India and China. We have publi
transportation that works and is readil
available. Over ninety percent of us have worl
and can support our families, so they are no
starving. In Canada, we have universal health
care, as does Europe, the UK, most of the G20.

We have so much to be grateful for, and we
are blessed.

Sometimes it is good to make up a

gratitude list when we don't think we have anything. Did you eat today? Did you sleep in a bed last night? Do you have a roof over your head, regardless of how humble it is? Do you have a friend or loved one that loves you, too?

Do you have work? Do you have an education? Are you in reasonable health? Can you practice the religion of your choice?

Can you change your social or economic standing by just making the decision that you want to? These are some very basic questions that a significant portion of the world's population can't answer affirmatively.

We in the Western world are indeed blessed. We can have whatever we want. If you are willing to pay the price and put in the effort, you can create any lifestyle you want. Good or bad. It's your choice. How do you create the lifestyle you want?

I try and take a few minutes out during the day and imagine I have already achieved what I want. I find this easy to do when I am going to bed at night. I see my children or speak to them on the phone or by Skype, and that makes me happy. Going for a walk along a country road in either eastern Ontario or the beautiful Sea Wall in Vancouver and imagine myself being able to

share with others my journey with the hope I ca
be of service to them creates a pleasant feelin
internally.

I imagine my children and grandchildren'
smiling faces because they've succeeded in thei
work. I see my creditors paid off.

We all have imagination. It is an excellen
tool to use. Creation gave it to us for a reasor
When we utilize our imagination, we can creat
mental images of what it is we desire.

This intellectual gift helps ou
subconscious mind in guiding us to take th
appropriate actions that help us produce th
results we desire.

It is a positive action to imagine yoursel
free of anxiety or unhealthy relationships if tha
is something that has plagued you due to you
upbringing or just life itself. But what about afte
you've done the work. Then what?

How about sitting on the beach in Mexico
if that's what you want? Imagine the white sand
beaches, the row upon row of palm tree
stretching out for miles and the sound of th
waves breaking against the shoreline. Imagine th
picturesque haciendas, all painted in paste
colors. Smell the glorious food cooking in th

restaurants. Hear the sounds of the Mariachi bands playing at dinner, the voices rising in beautiful melodic harmonies.

Imagine yourself with the person you wish you had a relationship with as you walk down the street. If there's someone you've met and you wish you could go out with him or her, imagine yourself out at dinner. See yourself laughing and relaxing in their company. Here, you can imagine that you ask them what they do. What do they like about life? What do they want out of life? What are their favorite activities? Who are their favorite authors, actors, and heroes? What's the single greatest moment or event in their life? When you are interested in others, people will find you attractive.

If you do meet the person and you find out that they have absolutely nothing in common with them, and it's the worst night of your life, give thanks for allowing you to see that this is not the right person to be out with at this time. It's in our attitudes how well we do with giving thanks.

I thank God every morning for another day. I happen to write to God every morning. It's something I started doing a quite a few years ago when I was having a problem imagining God, and I wanted a closer relationship with him/her. I was

still caught up in my confusion over my
Catholicism and whether or not I believed in the
divinity of Christ. I started to write God with the
idea that he was a friend of mine. It helped me to
create a personal relationship with a Higher
Power though I still don't know who or what God
is. I have journal upon journal that I've written
with all my letters. Some mornings I'm ranting
and raving, but most days I'm only thanking God
for all the blessings I have in my life today.

I often list my requests in those journals
and give thanks that I am being guided to take
the right actions. For instance, I have been
thinking about the whole process of Master
Minding. So here's my latest idea: I could set up
seminars for people who want to join in Master
Mind groups. Will this work? I have no idea.
could investigate and see if there is somewhere
we could host them.

Or I could contact Unity churches. I could
reach out to a Catholic Church, or the
Presbyterian Church, and see if they would allow
me to use space in the church to hold a seminar

I recently did a talk at the West Vancouver
United Church for a group of women, and it went
very well.

I begin imagining and seeing myself

delivering talks to groups of people. I probably won't fill halls in the beginning, but I might get twenty people out. A few years ago we did a Talking Peace seminar, where we had approximately fifty people attend. It was rewarding, and my only compensation was the good feeling I had that I was able to share my insights into what is going on in the world, because of my experience of creating that Counter-Terrorism series. The success was that we had fifty people contemplating the fact that they might be able to make a difference, regardless of the fact I was living on a small island at that time, far away from the centers of influence.

But I had a chance to see that my style of speaking and message got across. Where did I get it from? Before the evening started, I imagined I was guided in what was said. No one walked out angry or upset. As a matter of fact, some excellent ideas came out of the evening, and they want to do more of the talks. All of these experiences are leading to my career as an inspirational speaker and writer.

Another approach is to act as if you already have whatever it is you want. If you want to be a successful salesperson, or a successful commercial artist, a successful writer, a successful physician, a successful mother, a successful husband or parent, a successful aut technician, imagine yourself already in possession of it, and begin acting as if you alread have whatever it is you desire. How would you fee if you'd already received your request? You would feel happy, would you not? You would feel a rea sense of accomplishment. You would feel prou of yourself. You might try feeling grateful, too.

When I was a young producer and hadn' produced anything yet, people used to say to me "What do you do?" "I'm a producer," I would respond. "What have you produced?"

"I'm working on two projects right now. And I was, too. I'd bought the rights to a novel found, and I was working with Phillip on The Grey Fox and helping with the financing of Nails— getting him the money to finish paying off his creditors.

That's part of the job of producing Getting the money. I used to lie in bed at nigh and imagine having all the money in the bank but I always acted and spoke as if I was a producer. I did the same thing as a young record producer, too.

When we were making The Grey Fox, I used to sit and meditate and imagine having all the money, because we were having such a hard time raising the funds. I imagined the film finished, and I imagined it being successful. I saw us winning awards. I saw newspaper articles in my mind that were very positive.

I stopped doing that for several years, and I found myself back in the desert as a result. However, I recently went back and imagined positive press and critical reviews and awards on Yonge Street, Toronto Rock & Roll Stories. Ditto for The Gangster Next Door, which was the Canadian Broadcasting Corporation's second highest-rated documentary for 2011 and we were able to get the TV Magazine covers on Pagan Christ. I used this in a series we did for TLC and History Television called Counter Force, and it happened again.

We won the Gold Special Jury Award at Houston against twelve hundred other series that year. We received the Christopher Award too, where we competed against over a thousand entries. There are more, but I won't bore you with them. I know that imagining works. When I assume the feelings I would have if what I wanted came to me, then I am guided to take the right actions to accomplish my goals.

The human brain is the world's greatest

computer. It will guide you and give you answer
if you just give it the opportunity. When you
choose to use your Master Mind partner with it
the analogy is like loading sophisticated software
to get it working. If we ask it our subconscious
mind, it will always guide us and get us the right
answer. That's the voice of God—speaking
directly to us.

One way to utilize it is through meditation
Meditation is sitting quietly and listening. Prayer
allows me to talk to God and give him my
requests, and meditation allows me to sit back
and listen for God's reply.

When I slow my mind and relax and allow
all of the thoughts to pass through, then I open
myself up to experiencing the flow of power that
comes from a conscious contact with your higher
self. Here, we experience the feelings directly we
would have if our request were already present
Here we can get in touch with our inner self, our
unconscious mind, and allow it to give us the
knowledge we need to realize our desires. There
are many online or YouTube Guided Meditations
you can listen to by just going to Google and
typing in "Guided Meditation."

If your interest is in pursuing a life in the
arts or creativity, I can assure you that it is an

incredible experience to tap into the universal unconscious.

The late, great, Pierre Teilhard de Chardin, a Jesuit paleontologist involved in the discovery of the "Peking man," referred to it as "Cosmic Consciousness."

There exists around the earth a layer of super consciousness that every human being can tap into and utilize for our highest good to improve our conscious contact with God, and to receive inspiration and extraordinary insight.

It does allow you to grow and improve your chances of success exponentially. Meditation has several benefits to it. One is the apparent ability to access creativity. Intuition is increased, and we go toward projects, people, and outcomes that support our goals. We find ourselves inexplicably calm, too. We are plugged into a source of power and energy that is always available to everyone, but few take advantage of. Meditation does work to unlock the secrets of the ages as well. We will find ourselves receiving images and ideas that are quite profound and beautiful. The image I have is of a wave of tranquility, washing over us and leaving us refreshed and whole.

When I ask my unconscious for help solving a problem, and then take the time to

meditate, I am often given insights into th
problem other than the solution.

I see how my actions have led me there, an
what I might do in the future to avoid the sam
pitfalls.

I can have visions of my life as I would lik
it to be. I can see what it is I need to do, t
accomplish my desires. I am led to the usefu
ideas, people or institutions that will enable an
empower me to realize my worthy ideals. When
believe that God is responding, I assume th
feelings I would have if I accomplished my goal
It's as if I have uncovered a shortcut to m
desires. My unconscious cannot tell the rea
emotions from ones I choose to make up. But i
will react to them. When we say to ou
unconscious that we feel successful, it proceed
to help us attain whatever it is we think or tell i
we should have.

My unconscious does not have value
judgments like my conscious mind does. It simpl
enables me to operate in a way that creates wha
it is I'm thinking of at that time. That's why, if
harbor unconscious negative thoughts, my life i
filled with negative results a great deal of the time.
I don't understand why I feel this way. It's
because I'm totally unaware that I have these

feelings and thoughts, and I'm shocked when I wake up depressed or anxiety-ridden.

Giving thanks ensures more peace, more prosperity, more feelings of satisfaction and more of what it is we are giving thanks for. Giving thanks opens up a channel of receiving. It allows us to access God's grace in abundance. It enables me to expand my positive beliefs and experiences.

It is also important to give thanks when we are facing difficulties. Every obstacle carries with it the seed for equal or greater opportunity. When we are faced with stressful situations, we can either see them as problems, obstacles or challenges. I choose to take the path of a challenge and as my friend's Mary and Austin Hennessy, the ministers at Vancouver Unity Centre call them – Designer Moments to help us grow. When I give thanks for the difficulties in my life, I open the door to their solution. Inevitably, there is something I have to learn. I remind you of my story of Dixie Lanes. I thought my life was over. I thought I had to give up California, where I loved living. I had to give up my movie career to get better, which completely devastated me. I had to give up (I thought) who I was. Well, let's look at the reality of it.

An important realization I had was what if

I'd never come back to Toronto, I would neve have met the woman who became the mother c my two youngest children. She played significant role in my development as a huma being.

I would not have the beautiful children I d in my son, Brendan, and my daughter, Laurel.

I would not have renewed my relationshij with my children from my first marriage, Andrew and Colleen.

I probably wouldn't have cleaned up th wreckage of my former marriage, either. I would not have healed the relationship with my mothe and my family. I would not have been there to assist my mother in her greatest time of need. You can't put a price tag on that experience, or the healing power of all those elements.

The week I went back to Toronto in 1987 there were about five shootings on the Pacific Coast Highway in California. Fires raged through the canyons, and the hills started to all slide into the ocean. Many of my friends had to park four wheel drive vehicles facing out of the driveways so they could escape if a massive landslide started. Then they tore down the Malibu Coffee Shop and put up a nondescript mall. That made leaving easier. The fact is, I still visit LA regularly and I still love all of the beautiful things I can do in southern California. I love LA, as Randy Newman sang years ago, but I'm also happy at home in Canada.

When I had to give up my movie career, my stress level dropped significantly. I started to sleep after a few months, something I hadn't done in years.

I began to realize how unhealthy it was "being" what I did for a living. All of a sudden I went into a great depression, because I didn't have my ego identification anymore. Was that ever liberating when I realized I am not what I do for a living?

I have other interests, more than making movies or television. I love reading. I love skiing; I love working with others who are in need of help in their lives. I love teaching. I love writing. I like being a father. I loved being a husband. I loved being a volunteer fire fighter. I enjoyed working with the Amherst Island Men's Society (AIMS).

When I lived on Amherst Island, the people there couldn't care less whether or not I ever lived in Hollywood, New York, or Timmins for that matter. World-renowned neurosurgeons, writers, artists, former television anchors and stimulating farmers surrounded me on the Island. I was part

of a community of working people who buil
homes, work on roads and teach at Queen
University. I would have missed all of this if I'
stayed in California and never given up m
feature film producing. The fact is: I'd probab
be dead.

I can say the same today about Vancouve
and Toronto.

When I switched out of independent featur
films to television, I started to earn mone
consistently.

Sure, the chance to make millions wasn'
there unless I hit a home run on a series, but gon
were the incredible peaks and valleys.

My life became financially manageable.
didn't go another dime into debt, either until th
assault. Prior to that, I was coming out of debt.

And here's something I'd forgotten from m
early career. I liked making documentaries anc
series. I didn't have thirty-five different peopl
with their agendas telling us what to do. We wer
left alone, and I experienced more creativ
satisfaction than I ever had. It was fun. Wow
there's a concept. Doing something that's fun
instead of going out every day to get the crap
kicked out of you emotionally, mentally anc

physically.

I wouldn't have started teaching at two universities; I wouldn't have met all the interesting people I know today.

And think of this. I thought my life was over as I knew it when I lost everything because of Dixie Lanes. Dixie Lanes gave me my life back. It enabled me to see just how blessed I was, and what a complete fallacy it is to be totally caught up in a career where you sacrifice life to earn a living. So give thanks for difficulties. They will enable you to change the direction of your life, learn a lesson, and move on in a very positive way.

I would like to try and end child abuse by doing an independent documentary where I am not dependent on traditional broadcasters. I would like to do for child abuse what Vice President Gore did for Climate Change. But whether I get it made or not, it's not going to define who I am or what it is I'm all about. It will simply be that we are creating entertainment that just might help change the world for the better.

Giving Thanks allows me to obtain more of life. Giving thanks for what we have enables us to experience God's abundance in all areas of our lives. Acting as if we have already received what we're asking for speeds up the process of getting

it. There's an old spiritual axiom that works: Fak
it until you make it. It works. It does.

18. I DEDICATE MY LIFE – STEP EIGHT

I Dedicate My Life: I now have a covenant in which it is agreed that the Master Mind is supplying me with an abundance of all things necessary to live a successful and happy life. I dedicate myself to be of maximum service to God and those around me; to live in a manner that sets the highest example for others to follow, and to remain responsive to God's guidance. I go forth with a spirit of enthusiasm, excitement and expectancy. I am at peace.

I can hardly believe that we've arrived here at the last of the eight steps. This process started the first week of May 2001. As I write this, it is March 14, 2016. Almost fifteen years since I began it.

But God supplied me with an abundance of energy and dedication to get this book finished. Here is the greatest single leap of faith I will take with these steps. Either God is, or God isn't. I choose to believe S/He is.

Then I either am willing to release my life

entirely to God's direction and care, realizing tha I will be given everything I need to live a success filled and happy life, or I will continue

living on unhealthy, self-defeating and self directed thinking that often generates fear and confusion in my life.

And almost all of it comes out of ou childhoods. It is time to let it go and thank th little guy or gal inside of you for trying to protec you. It is the five to ten-year old you making se many of the decisions that keep creating the confusion, fear, anger, resentment, and chaos in your life.

Self-reliance does work, some of the time We just pay an awful price for it. But if you're one of those individuals who views the way of life I'm suggesting as wimpy, boring, phony, or any of the other views I once held about it, then I just wish you happiness. I want to meet someone who has lived his or her life totally on self-direction achieving all their material goals, amassing fabulous riches and lying on their deathbed saying, "I wish I'd spent more time at the office." I don't think that's a success-filled and happy life It is one full of money and power, but it also tends to be a lonely one. We have to sacrifice so much to gain that material wealth—if that is all we are after. I know the rewards are very short-lived.

I realize there are many very successful people, by the way, who have been able to create a balance.

That is, they acknowledge that it is the Divine Universe's guidance and love that has enabled them to be so prosperous, but they also tend to have very balanced lives at home and in their spare time. They create opportunities to contribute back to life.

They spend time with their families. They give back to their community. They can give of their time, money and love. That's the key. What are we giving back to life when we're in the midst of getting so much?

You may ask the question: what is a successful and happy life? To me, it is the realization of any worthy ideal. If I want a happy and joyous family life, free of fear of the past, anger in the present with enough money to meet our current needs and put away some for savings, then that is a beginning. But what else might there be?

Well, what about a deeper, more meaningful relationship with your Higher Power? One, where you can let go of worry about the future. How about a life where you can release your childhood, family your finances? Imagine being free of worry about your relationship or your marriage? Wouldn't it be wonderful to release your children or loved ones to the God of your understanding's care? You wouldn't have to give it another thought as far as trying to control, fix or manipulate how it's going to turn out.

When we can live peace-filled and happy lives, as the result of what we are doing in our daily lives, we are successful. When our children love us, when we contribute to our communities, we are living happy and prosperous lives. When we think of the needs of others in a healthy way, not a codependent way, we are living happy and peaceful lives. When we can either donate our time, energy or resources to helping those less fortunate, we are living happy and prosperous lives.

When you build a birdhouse, a garage or a house that you've always wanted, then you're living a happy and successful life. When you get the car of your dreams, or the boat or the fishing rod you've always wanted, you're living a fruitful and happy life. When you take time out to speak to someone you would not normally talk to and honestly, inquire how they are, and listen to what they have to say, you are living a successful and happy life.

There is no limit to what you can want and have. Travel, excitement, and exploration are all worthy pursuits. Education—regardless of what age you are—is a wonderful journey. Trying to learn how to play the violin, piano, or guitar creates a successful life if you can play one tune. To me, that is what we can expect when we dedicate our lives to our Higher Power.

You can expect to have enough. It is God's pleasure to give you the kingdom. All you have to do is ask. It is important to remember, however, that when we ask only for ourselves, it won't be as satisfying. But having a covenant, which is a sacred agreement or contract, enables all of us to obtain peace in our lives. Happiness in itself is not something we can generate.

Happiness to me is a by-product of doing something well. It is the gift that comes with giving. Happiness is achievable when we reach a goal, help a friend, give to the community, or seek God's will in our lives. Peace is created by the absence of fear or conflict. That is achieved when we relinquish our worries and doubts to God. Peace comes when we've done the best we can in any situation and let go of the results. Peace is an unearned gift.

Of course, for most of us, we continuall
worry about how our lives will work out because
while we want to believe, we may have lingerin
doubts.

That's okay, too. But after a period, i
becomes evident that when we try and work ou
lives in agreement with our Higher Power's plan
life just has a way of working out. It means tha
we can begin living spiritual lives and, in som
cases, we might want to start living a religious lif
too. But having a covenant with God enables al
of us to develop our personal relationship with th
God of your understanding that supports us ir
our endeavors.

I think God cares about what is in ou
hearts. Do we want to be of service? Do we hav
love in our heart? Are we mean-spirited, critical
impatient or judgmental at home? Do we try t
find a resolution that works for the greatest goo
and the greatest number of life's problems? Ir
traffic, when we go nuts and give someone th
finger, do we try and get them to open thei
window and apologize for our behavior? Do w
readily admit when we've made a mistake? Car
we forgive those who've harmed us? Are w
willing to put ourselves out to help someone tha

may need my assistance because they are differently abled?

To me, these are questions that carry much more weight than what does my outward appearance look like to someone. These are the standards that I believe God holds me to, and that people want to know about the real me. I want to be clear. I think my Higher Power loves me in spite of my flaws. I don't believe I will ever have the kind of saintliness of a Mother Theresa. That's why she deserved to be sainted. I'm no saint. You can take that to the bank.

But that doesn't stop me from trying to act in a decent way. I just recognize that most of my life will have certain struggles in it. I'd love to believe that all of my imperfections will be removed someday.

It's nice to think of myself as this calm, peaceful guy who will sit around dispensing wisdom and knowledge with incense burning while we sip tea. Those who know me can now get off the floor from laughing. Probably not going to happen, they're saying. But I'm okay with that because I believe the Diving Presence loves me just the way I am. I dispense love and whatever wisdom I've acquired from my local coffee shop, where I often find myself in my deepest and most meaningful conversations.

The most sincere desire I have today is t
be of maximum service to God and those aroun
me. I can't believe I'm writing that, but it is tru
today. When I work with a Master Mind grou
week after week, I begin to see the miracles tha
get manifested in our lives. We experience ou
requests, being granted. We see that we are give
the tools to handle difficult situations at home
We can be present when our loved ones get sic
or die.

I want to tell you about our late friend, Bil
Bill was a retired psychiatrist. He had the prot
evolution symbol on the back of his car—the on
that has a fish and underneath it reads "Darwin,
with the fish evolving legs. Bill prayed every weel
with Richard and me for almost eight years
While he never came to a place of accepting tha
there was an anthropomorphic being—the bi
guy in the sky—he did come to see the value o
prayer and the value of fellowship.

Richard figured out that we had over 60(
lunches with Bill. When Bill was laying in the
hospital dying, both Richard and I would visi
him, and we'd sit there and pray for him, and you
know, no one knew he was going to go—but when
he did, he was very, very peaceful. Odd for a mar

who was a trained medical scientist; first as a doctor, then an anesthesiologist, then a trained psychiatrist who suggested that while he didn't clearly understand how prayer worked when he did pray, he just felt better. He was the one who was a power of example for me to pray for humility, clarity of thought and peace of mind. Bill was the humblest human being I've ever known—and one of the most spiritual, in spite of being an agnostic.

When we try to be and are of maximum service to others, we find that we are given the answers to problems that in the past may have totally mystified us.

As a result of our dysfunctional childhoods, quite often in life, we find ourselves confronted by interpersonal relations that don't go well. We have mutual friends who participate in gossip. When we find ourselves getting sucked into the vortex of personalities, it is difficult to extract ourselves unless we've taken the high road, right off the top and done the spiritual work to realize when we gossip we open ourselves up to be gossiped about by others.

The law of cause and effect does exist. Here's an example of where our covenant supplies us with the spiritual resolve to not get into this form of character assassination.

One great question I heard from someon
about gossip was: "Is what you're about to tell m
going to contribute in any significant way to m
or another person's life?"

The obvious answer is "No," and it tends t
stop people in their tracks. I suppose the way w
address the issue with them will have
significant bearing on the outcome. If I sham
them for their actions versus pointing out to then
with love the potential harm their words ma
cause, the solution may prove more harmful tha
the problem. When we choose to help our fellov
travelers, we are given a sense of peace anc
happiness.

We find ourselves elevated above these life
draining experiences. We are of maximum servic
when we try and act in a positive way.

I used to batter people over the head with th
truth, under the mistaken belief I was helpin
them.

There are times, however—and this i
where discernment comes in—when you have tc
get someone's attention with a two by four.

When people are self-deluded about

perceived harm is done to them, or they, believe they are being picked on, when the fact is, it is their self-centeredness that is really at the cause of some issue, drastic action is sometimes necessary. It's a question of your relationship with them. I find a direct, but loving, statement to use. "I know you believe that you were wronged, but I must tell you that I think your ego is out of control."

You might want to ask their permission to share with them your insight. If they say "No," then back off. Life will give them the same message. It may not be as gentle, however.

Our covenant guarantees that we will be able to survive any difficulty life may throw at us with dignity and grace. There is a real sense of satisfaction and happiness to be gained by being a power of example for people going through adversity. If most of your life you've been someone who has been emotionally out of control, someone people have had to assist constantly, think of the reaction of others when you can be there for them. If we accept our covenant with God, then we can support those in need, without needing anything for ourselves. I am reminded of the prayer of St. Francis. This prayer is a great philosophy to live by regardless of our faith.

Lord, make me a channel of Thy peace, that where there is hatred I may bring love; that where there is wrong, I may bring a spirit of forgiveness; that where there is discord, I may bring harmony; that where there is error, I may bring truth; that where there is doubt, I may bring faith; that where there is despair, I may bring hope; that were there are shadows, I may bring light; that where there is sadness, I may bring joy. Lord, grant that I may seek to comfort rather than to be comforted; to understand, than to be understood; to love, than to be loved. For it is by self-forgetting, that one finds peace. It is by forgiving, that one is forgiven. And it is by dying, that one awakens to Eternal Life. Amen.

If I choose to live my life by one simple spiritual belief, then I suppose that this prayer is the one to try and live it by. Some years ago, when I was working on my codependency, I hated this prayer. I thought it was incredibly unhealthy. I spoke volumes to me about losing myself in others' problems, of not taking care of myself.

As I've grown and changed, I've begun to see the strong elements of this prayer. Francis was an interesting young man when he entered religious life. He gave up a great deal. He had everything a person could want. He had a good family, good prospects, and wealth.

He yearned to be of service. I see when I am healthy, when I have the knowledge that can make a difference when I subjugate my ego, I am given great rewards.

St. Francis' prayer is a recipe for peace of mind and happiness. It is also one of the most difficult spiritual disciplines to try and live by because it is in complete contradiction to my ego-based existence. But it contains the seeds of true joy.

In March 1970, I lay in a horrible room of an acquaintance of mine that was painted all black. I was renting this room from him when I split up with my first wife. I was speaking to a friend on a telephone because, for the first time, I was seriously in trouble and I knew it. I couldn't get free of alcohol. This friend started to repeat the Prayer of St. Francis with me, and I was suddenly catapulted into the fourth dimension. I had a profound spiritual awakening. To this day, I've never had a drink. I was 22 years old at that time. The problem was in my faulty thinking. I couldn't surrender my old thinking and my absolute desire only to get what I wanted for me. But I recognized there was power in that prayer. It epitomizes the best in spiritual goals.

I trust today that I am being guided. I feel

a sense of excitement about the future. I am fille
with a sense of hope that I will be able to be
service to others, and create some dramati
changes in my life. I expect my life to work out.
expect to be able to do my inspirational talks, an
I hope that I will be blessed for my efforts.

In the same way, I expect that I will have t
deal with issues from time to time in my life tha
will cause me great pain and suffering. That's th
way life is. I know I will be guided to the righ
people, places, and solutions. I believe and affirn
that I am being guided to the right people, th
right opportunities and the right results in m
life.

In spite of the uncertainty I am under at th
moment due to my injury, I expect great things ir
my future. I expect that my children will do well
I expect that I will be able to overcome al
difficulties in life with God's help.

I expect that I will receive sufficient fund
to repay my old creditors. I sincerely hope tha
anyone I've harmed in the distant past will forgiv
me, and in turn, I will forgive any who hav
harmed me.

I expect good health for my family and me
I expect prosperity. I expect to have a peace-fillec
and happy life. It doesn't matter whether I wil

ever produce another movie or television show in my life. I will be led to the right people and projects, as long as my intentions are to be of service.

I want to close off this book with a story about pain. I've always wondered why, if there were a God, he would allow people to die and suffer what I perceived to be needless.

Here's what I've come to realize. I don't know why some people need to die prematurely or suffer, but what I've come to realize is that for some, pain is integral to their growth and eventual transformation.

When my son Brendan was born, he was born with 180-degree clubfeet. The poor little guy was heading north, and his feet were going south. When he was six days old, I had to take him to the Hospital for Sick Children in Toronto. The surgeon told me to hold him down on the large metal examining table as he looked at his feet.

Now here was my newborn son, a week old, and I'm sure that his small, undeveloped brain understood only warmth, being dry and feeding. All he felt was love and comfort. But when I laid him on that table, and the doctor took his little feet and twisted them right around one hundred and eighty degrees so he could put plaster casts on his legs to help straighten them out, all thi poor baby knew was that he was in agony.

My brain is like little Brendan's when i comes to trying to understand God, or his pla for me, or anyone else. All Brendan was capabl of was feeling the pain.

He didn't understand the concept o healing. Week after week, I kept bringing Brenda back to that hospital, and week after week, h would scream in agony, and the tears

would stream down my face because I loved hin so much I wasn't willing to let him go through lif physically disabled.

I subjected him to that experience for ove six months. Then he had to have a very painfu operation where they cut each foot from one sid to the other so they could cut around the back o his heels from mid-foot to mid-foot on the othe side. Then they sliced his tendon in half on eacl foot to stretch them. Then they drove steel pin: through the back of his heels to hold his fee straight. By the time he was nine months old, he could recognize the doorway to Sick Children' Hospital in Toronto, and he would just start to shake and sob.

He couldn't understand that he needed the

pain to change how his feet were pointing, so that today, he walks and runs normally. No one would ever know unless I told this story that he was born technically disabled.

Pain is the touchstone of change in our lives. I don't know why I have to endure the pain of life at times. All I know is when I do, and it ends, I'm always better off than I was.

That will probably be true until the day I die. I don't know why people die in mass numbers in natural catastrophes. I don't know why planes crash into buildings, into the ocean, into homes. I don't know why young children die. That is one of the great mysteries to me.

Like Brendan, I just cannot figure it out, but undoubtedly I will one day. Until then, I look forward to each day, and all the amazing adventures and challenges I will face and overcome. I look forward to being able to meet some of you as I trudge the road to happy destiny.

God bless you, and may you find your path to healing, freedom and reclaiming your life

ABOUT THE AUTHOR

David Brady's work is best known in Canada but no stranger to U.S. and European audiences. He's been the President of four film and television production companies. But his road to success was filled with childhood trauma, heartache, substance abuse and massive debt. He revisited his past to exorcise those demons in his inspirational autobiography, "Transforming Childhood Trauma, 8 Steps To Reclaim Your Life!

Brady's film and television projects have won numerous awards two Golden Globe nominations including Best Foreign Film and Best Actor for "The Grey Fox," presented by Francis Ford Coppola's Zoetrope Studios and released through United Artists Classics. His other Canadian and American television awards are too numerous to mention.

David holds an MFA from York University in Toronto and was an undergraduate and graduate student at Simon Fraser University in Vancouver, British Colombia. Brady was also on the faculties of York University and Ryerson University in Toronto, where he was the recipient of the CESAR teaching award. Most recently he taught Introductory Screenwriting at Capilano University in Vancouver, British Columbia.

His recent book, Aging With Dignity, Living With Grace continues to garner five out of five-star reviews.

Please feel free to email any questions or comments to davidbradybooks@gmail.com

Made in the USA
Charleston, SC
07 April 2016